# Spendsmart

# Spendsmart

## How to tackle debt, know your money mind and make your cash go further

### Jay Hunt and Benjamin Fry

PIATKUS

PIATKUS

First published in Great Britain in 2009 by Piatkus Books

A CIP catalogue record for this book
is available from the British Library

ISBN 978-0-7499-2999-2

Design by Grounded Design
Typeset in Charter ITC by Action Publishing Technology Ltd, Gloucester
Printed and bound in Great Britain by Clays Ltd, St Ives plc

Papers used by Piatkus are natural, renewable and recyclable
products made from wood grown in sustainable forests and certified
in accordance with the rules of the Forest Stewardship Council.

Mixed Sources
Product group from well-managed
forests and other controlled sources
www.fsc.org  Cert no. SGS-COC-004081
© 1996 Forest Stewardship Council
FSC

Piatkus Books
An imprint of
Little, Brown Book Group
100 Victoria Embankment
London EC4Y 0DY

An Hachette Livre UK Company
www.hachettelivre.co.uk

www.piatkus.co.uk

*To Benjamin – for keeping my head together during long filming days on Spendaholics.*

*To Jay – the real inspiration behind this book and for showing me the ropes on Spendaholics.*

# CONTENTS

# Introduction

More than ever before, making the right money choices is paramount.

If you are badly in debt, we know what a difficult place that is to be; if you want help to keep better tabs on where you spend your money then the exercises within this book will give you honest answers; if you find that others have a better lifestyle than you, yet they are on the same salary, we can help you to become more aware of making the right spending choices; and if you want to understand what drives you to overspend in the first place, be prepared to uncover some interesting psychological insights.

## The Spendsmart experts

### Jay Hunt

I got into debt myself in my twenties, so I know what an effort it can be to change your spending patterns and dig yourself out of that hole. I have worked with a lot of overspenders who needed to get out of the red fast, and that's why my practical, tried-and-tested approach is full of hands-on advice for any financial situation. So whether you are struggling with student debt, remortgaged up to the hilt, over your limit on credit cards or feeling squeezed by rising living costs and clueless as to where your salary actually goes every month, my insider tips are guaranteed to work.

In this book you'll find spending guides that reveal how you can get the most from your cash, creative ideas to help you stick to your budget, as well as the Spendsmart Directory at the end, so you need never waste a penny again.

## Benjamin Fry

I provide psychological expertise coupled with no-nonsense insight. My Spendsmart advice looks at how you can automatically stop spending simply by understanding your own spending personality, and my practical guides are there to help you through each of the five Spendsmart steps.

Overspenders are people who are using destructive patterns of behaviour to communicate something. The big questions are what, and to whom? To help answer these, I have included in-depth case studies throughout the book, illustrating how I have transformed the minds of real-life debtors. As you work through the plan I will help *you* to find your own personal answers, and in so doing, will provide you with a whole new strategy for getting underneath the cause of your self-destructive spending.

## Our experience

We have pooled our joint experience from working with private clients and those we have helped on Spendaholics, our hit BBC3 show, to formulate a down-to-earth approach that works. Our methods have been proven beyond a doubt to be a huge success with debt-ridden and insolvent individuals from all walks of life. Our extensive experience makes us ideally placed to put you firmly back on your financial feet, stop any overspending, help you develop an understanding of your own shopping psyche, free you from compulsive shopping habits and get you back on track.

Without lecturing, patronising or insisting on a lifetime of self-denial, Spendsmart is both empathetic and effective, allowing you to make the most of every penny in your pocket. Use it as your money handbook, an invaluable tool you can take to your bank manager to back you up, a manual on how not to get ripped off, or a credit crunch survival guide. It is designed to be a handbook you can refer to again and again for any, or all, of your money matters.

## How to do Spendsmart

Spendsmart is a simple five-step plan. The steps are packed with practical advice and sound psychological pointers guaranteed to stop your overspending, explore issues around why you spend the way you do and provide you with a set of solutions to follow, whatever your personal circumstances. Whether you are looking for tips on how to survive a global economic crisis, a better understanding of your money mind, or a need to make your cash go further, we are here to help you.

Each chapter should be closely followed, and, with the exception of Step Three (a seven-day plan), there are no restrictions as to how long each step should take you to complete. Everyone is different and some steps may take you longer than others. However, the important thing is that you do them in the time frame that feels right for you. The only rule is that you do the steps in order. After all, there is not much point in jumping to Step Four in which you need to put a budget together if you have not bothered to learn more about your spending habits in the previous three steps. It just won't work!

In addition, at the end of the book you will find the Spendsmart Directory. This provides links and contacts that correspond to each of the five steps in the book, so that you have the most up-to-date information and resources at your fingertips. Refer to it and use it as you go along, to help you on your journey to becoming Spendsmart.

# The Spendsmart five

## Step One – Spendsmart reality

This is where we work out what has actually gone wrong with your spending and examine where you are right now and how you got to this point. We also take a reality check on your emotional relationship with money, help you deal with your money realities and provide a comprehensive set of solutions for preventing your debts and money issues from getting any worse.

## Step Two – Spendsmart preparation

The key to money success is in the planning and in finding the motivation and courage this requires. This is where we get you to clear the decks, sort out your living space and start to study in detail how your bad spending habits can be reversed so that you are ready to do the Spendsmart detox in a calm and positive way that will ensure success.

## Step Three – Spendsmart detox

This seven-day plan is designed to get you to focus on where you really spend and understand the emotions you are masking by doing so. It will reveal how you can live on less than you think, examine what you miss and what you don't, show

how you respond to living on a budget and expose your money moods. What you learn about yourself and your spending habits during your detox will ensure you stay on track throughout the rest of the Spendsmart process. You will be able to create new personal spending rules, find substitutes for spending and be aware of areas of temptation for the future – shopping knowledge is power.

## Step Four – Spendsmart budget

This is where all your hard work pays off. Using all the knowledge you have gained about yourself in the previous steps we take you through a process of setting up a budget that you can stick to, based on your own choices and personal situation. By now you will recognise where your emotional triggers are and be equipped to deal with them.

## Step Five – Spendsmart life

There will always be times in life when spending can get out of control, and times when it's important to be able to make the right money choices. Step Five is a brilliant in-the-know chapter designed to keep your money matters simple and your bank balance thriving, no matter what your situation. From your wardrobe and your home, through to birthdays, holidays and Christmas, it covers anything you might need to spend on, showing you where and how to make savings. Used in conjunction with the Directory at the end of the book, it is the perfect guide to life for the new Spendsmart you!

# Will Spendsmart work for you?

Being open-minded about the fact that spending is probably not the whole story, along with a willingness to look at your life as a whole are intrinsic to our plan. In our experience, the more you are willing to explore your life holistically rather than looking at your spending issues in isolation, the more likely you are to succeed. You want to triumph over your money problems by understanding their roots and we want to motivate you to change and to be strong enough to turn any adjustments into permanent lifestyle changes. This will allow you to take on board all the practical tips and tricks we offer so that you can get a grip on your issues and in the case of bad debts, stop any further actions.

If you want to know if Spendsmart can help you out just ask yourself:

- How do you spend your money today?
- Does it make you happy?
- Do you feel miserable even though you know you live in an affluent society?
- Do you feel that the more you earn the more things you need to buy?
- Do you struggle to understand what is behind your urge to spend?
- Do you worry about your ability to live on less?

It does not matter how you got into financial trouble or what you spend your money on, the Spendsmart plan is for everyone. All of us spend in different ways, on different things and in massively different amounts. Ultimately, more of us than ever are getting into debt younger, so we know that help is needed.

## The Spendsmart guarantee

Our promise to you is that by following the Spendsmart plan with us you will:

- be unafraid when opening bills and statements
- feel OK about checking your bank balance
- be in control of your money when you hit the high street
- know about how you can pay less for more
- formulate solid plans to get you through a credit crunch
- be able to afford the things you really want
- no longer be tempted to buy things you don't need
- be happier while spending less
- be free from that spending guilt the second after you make a purchase
- rethink relationships that are costing you dear
- feel empowered and free from spending shame
- be able to create a home free from useless clutter
- be able to identify the roots of your spending behaviour
- understand the emotional pitfalls that undermine smart spending.

## Getting started

We already know that you want to sort out your money problems, so now let's get on with it. We will be with you every step of the way on your Spendsmart journey, offering support, sharing with you the experiences of others and providing practical tips. Whether your spending weakness is clothes, your kids or your car, we have seen it all before and are old hands at addressing your thrill at the till – a tipping point for many people to take back control.

Perhaps most importantly of all, however, Spendsmart will empower you, giving you the courage to change for ever.

# STEP ( 1 ) ONE

# Spendsmart Reality

Step One of Spendsmart is called 'reality' and is exactly what it says. Looking at your spending reality is crucial to the success of the Spendsmart plan as it helps you to understand your own situation. We will work with you to help you to understand the reasons why you have been an overspender, come to terms with the reality of how much you owe today, and put in place some immediate solutions to prevent your problems from getting any worse.

## Where are you at?

Before we work out where you are at with your money it's worth taking a look at how you got there.

For some, a credit card spree, a massive mortgage or a life-long passion for cars might be the obvious reason for ending up in debt, but for others it is not that simple. Debt can creep up on you over a number of years and it is vital that we explore the causes that are relevant to your particular situation.

Spendsmart reality is going to centre on:

- You and only you
- Your money
- Your decisions
- Your feelings.

So take a minute and consider the following list of questions:

- Do you avoid opening your bank statements and credit card bills?
- Do you worry endlessly about money?
- Do you owe friends or family money?
- Do you lie to your friends and family about your debts?
- Do you feel out of control with your spending?
- Do you mentally spend next month's salary before you've even got it?
- Do you worry that you have no savings?
- Do you owe money on store cards and credit cards with high interest rates?
- Do you think that understanding money matters is just too boring?
- Do you worry that an unexpected bill like a house or car repair bill could mean you go under?
- Do you think that you can run up huge debts now and pay them off when you are older?
- Do you feel that although you have no money, you deserve a treat?
- Do you think that something or someone else is going to come along and sort out your money issues for you?
- Have you missed monthly payments on your mortgage, rent or credit cards?
- Can you remember when your monthly salary last got you through a whole month?

- Do you think it's pointless to even try to sort out your money and debts?
- Do you ever think that if it all gets too much you will just declare yourself a bankrupt and write your debts off?

If the answer to *any* of the above questions is 'Yes', chances are you are very much in need of some Spendsmart advice.

## The overspending syndrome

Shopping has become a favourite hobby for many of us, and shopping centres the world over are filled with classic over-spenders.

We buy things when we know we shouldn't: we spend money on cool clothes for our children that they will inevitably ruin in no time, we spend way too much on designer jeans for ourselves that don't even really fit and we buy flash cars on hire-purchase deals when we know we can't afford to run them. Somehow, though, we always manage to convince ourselves that our spending is worth it, in the hope that *this* time we have bought the ultimate magic-fix item – one that makes us happy, that means we never want to spend on anything again, one that we never get sick of and that totally changes our life for the better.

But guess what? That magic-fix item simply does not exist. You might feel for five minutes that this time you have really found it, but somehow it never completes your life, so off you go again on yet another fruitless search, guaranteed to fail, and each time costing you more and more and more. If this sounds familiar, don't be alarmed; we have heard it all before from people who thought they would never stop spending but have now turned their lives around.

Spending is not about simple economics. Why we overspend on some items and not others can be hard to work out. The old-fashioned ideal of going out to buy something with just enough money in our pockets like our parents did is just not what happens any more. Today, it's not only the basics that matter but all the other things we *think* we need – exfoliators, iPod accessories, digital TV, Internet connections, organic blueberries, dry leg moisturisers, designer buggies, new sunglasses, etc.

If you have been an overspender you will need to identify and break your compulsive spending patterns. If you recognise any of the feelings described below when you are out shopping then we have work to do and we will be looking at ways to do it later in this chapter.

## Recognising a compulsive spending pattern

The shopping scenario outlined here demonstrates clearly the various stages of classic overspending behaviour.

### 1. Your brain engages

You spot the handbag, speaker system, dining table you can't live without and start to imagine that item in your life – how fantastic it would be, how it would make you feel, how it would solve all your problems. You just have to have that magical item.

### 2. Justification

Your brain supplies you with all the reasons why you *should* have this item – you have worked so hard, you had a big row with your partner this morning, you feel unappreciated at work, you feel fat or simply that you deserve a treat and this is it.

## 3. Adrenalin starts pumping

This is when you feel the kick, the dilemma. Should I buy it? It's over my budget. Which card do I have credit on? Can I really purchase something so expensive? I can't believe I am actually going to do this . . .

## 4. Denial

All thoughts of your bank balance go out of your head; you know you are going to make this purchase and you don't want to feel bad.

## 5. Purchase

You hand over the card (rarely are these purchases made with cash), you punch in your PIN, your heart rate starts to slow and by the time you are given the bag or receipt for the goods, your spending hit is over.

## 6. Remorse

You leave the shop and it is now that you feel really bad. You remember how big your overdraft is and are aware of having broken a promise to yourself to not spend. You start to panic and think that maybe you should take the item back when you realise that you don't even know the store's returns policy. You feel ashamed and may well decide to hide the item when you get home; you just can't cope with dealing with it yet.

# What sort of overspender are you?

It is really important for you to look at the areas in which you have been an overspender.

If you are overspending on your rent or mortgage you may have to consider renting out a room or moving to somewhere you can afford to run while you repay your debts. If it is supermarket bills, you might need to think about a new way of eating and shopping that will allow you to stay within budget. If all your money is going on your utilities bills, have you done everything you can to insulate your house? Does your money go on entertaining or socialising? If so, how can you still have fun and money in your pocket?

Whatever your overspending habits have been, you need to start identifying them right now in this Spendmsart reality step before we can move on to doing something about them.

## Have you been overspending too soon?

Think about what happens when you get your pay cheque. Do you have a list of things that it is going to pay for before it even hits your account? Overspenders often find that they only have a few days of the month in the black when their salary gets paid in – debts, credit card bills and all the new things they want to buy can mean their account is cleared out in a number of days.

If you can't remember a time when your salary actually lasted a whole month and find that every month you end up owing more than the month before without a clue as to where the money has gone, you need to go through your statements and work out the areas you overspend in.

## Have you been overspending abroad?

You can't understand the exchange rate so you just blank it out and shop; after all, holidays are a time for treats, great wine, dinners out and anything else you fancy. You have bills for shopping in duty free. You feel free from debt worries in a new place and end up buying things you would never even look at if you were at home . . .

Think about how long it will take you to pay off all these holiday debts and consider giving yourself a holiday budget in pounds – you just need to do one exchange calculation and know that is your total for the holiday. Then take that amount with you in traveller's cheques and know that when it has gone, that is it until you get home. Also, make yourself a mini exchange rate card listing different amounts converted into the currency you will be using and keep it in your wallet for easy reference.

## Have you been overspending on others?

Does having a few drinks make you overgenerous? Are you the one everyone loves to go out drinking with, always the first to get a round in and often making a grand gesture of footing the bill to show off? Are you the one who turns up to a birthday party with a present that makes others gasp in admiration? Do you love taking your children shopping or treating your mum?

No one would guess you had money problems the way you shop. You like to do it with a flourish and spending on others gives you real pleasure. Generosity is a great quality but you should think about doing something for your friends and family that does not involve money. Try giving of your time, for example, rather than giving in ways that you cannot sustain.

## Have you been overspending at the sales?

Are you the sort of person who cannot resist a bargain? The minute you see a sale sign you blank out anything else at all. Your home and your wardrobe are full of great sale bargains that are somehow never as good as they were in the shop once you get them through your own front door.

Sales mean that things that are normally out of your price range are suddenly within it, opening up a whole new world to you. But unless you can pay off the credit card bill at the end of the month those items will end up costing you more than they would have done at full price. Do remember that sales are full of things the shops can't get rid of, so although it's a good opportunity to buy a new fridge or vacuum cleaner, it's not such a good opportunity to buy things for your wardrobe, unless you are replacing an item that is worn out.

## Have you been overspending on quantity not quality?

Are you a discount-store junkie? Are you only really happy if you can pile it all up at the till and go home with dozens of items for very little? Do you boast to your friends about how much you've bought and what a huge bargain it was, yet somehow never seem to have anything you really treasure?

What you are doing is convincing yourself that the items you've bought were so cheap that it does not matter. But it does. The adrenalin rush that these not-so-small-but-often shopping trips deliver is not enough to keep you away from the shops for long, so you go back, spend more and keep going round in circles. You are just shopping for shopping's sake, to get a quick fix. Beware of your addiction stores and avoid them. Think about having fewer quality items that you cherish, rather than lots of cheaper items that you tire of fast.

## Have you been overspending on impulse buys?

Do you leave the office to get some lunch and come back with a new pair of shoes, five CDs or a couple of books? This is an automatic see-and-spend pattern which can be a hard habit to break. If you find yourself fidgeting and feeling impatient in the queue to pay, you're probably desperate to spend and move on to the next fix, which is a good sign you've been overspending on impulse buys.

Try going out with just enough cash for that sandwich, or only going into a shop when you have a list of things that you need – shampoo, dog food, etc. It may be a boring list, but getting a buzz from buying lots of small things you don't need is a real waste of your money; at least this way you are spending on items you actually need.

## Have you been overspending to fill emotional needs?

Do you hit the shops as a way to escape? Does a row with your partner, the kids driving you mad or your boss refusing you a promotion send you into a frenzy of comfort buying? Spending when you are in this mood is never going to work and you will only ever be punishing yourself. The purchases you make will end up reminding you of the situation that you were trying to blank out in the first place, so that you don't want to use or wear them in any case.

You need to find alternative responses to these feelings so that you don't end up using shopping as a form of therapy.

## Benjamin – understanding your own spending history

As we have seen, overspending is not just about money. Clearly, it is the product of a relationship between a person and his or her money. Yet this relationship aspect of personal finances is often overlooked because so many of the details that make up a financial overview tend to be practical and impersonal. But at the heart of every overspent situation is an overspender – a person, not just a bank balance. So it's important to spend time considering not just *what* you spend, but *why* you spend.

If you are an overspender you spend more than you should one decision at a time, and it is the financial consequence of a series of these decisions that leads to trouble. So to get to the root of the problem we need to look at what each of these decisions represents, and why each one is taken.

In our experience of working with overspenders we have seen an alarming array of spending choices, as varied as the people who make them. However, they all seem to share one core issue: people choosing to spend money that they should not be spending, and somehow getting through that spending moment by short-circuiting the part of their mind that knows it is a bad idea.

So what's going on? We know that we need to look both ways when crossing the road. Our brains will not allow us to walk out into a busy road without looking, or only looking one way. Why then are we so reckless and self-destructive with our money? The answer seems to lie in an intricate concept we formulate of what money really means to us and what it represents.

# CASE STUDY

Helen works in a high-maintenance industry. She watches the world of fashion and glamour going on all around her, but as a PA she has a limited salary and, therefore, limited financial resources. However, she is seduced into the lifestyle of her bosses – eating out, drinking champagne, never saying no. The result is that she backs herself into a corner, unable to give up the life that she is 'enjoying', while simultaneously worrying herself sick over the debt.

It's easy to look at Helen and say, 'Oh well, she's only got herself to blame. She's had her fun and now she must pay the price.' But she knows that, and yet she can't stop. Surely then, there must be more to the story? What would be going on for Helen in that one moment when she'd be making a purchase?

Through analysis of Helen as a person in a relationship with money – leaving the rest of her life to one side – the process was broken down, moment by moment, as she spent money that she couldn't afford. Helen realised that far from being either a simple transaction or something she did without thinking, there was an emotional side to her spending. When asked what that was, she agreed that it was a rebellion, almost an act of defiance.

But most surprising was why she was rebelling, or, more specifically, against whom. Helen immediately said this was her parents, even though they had been dead for over five years. She was angry about various choices they had made on her behalf when she was younger, but had never had a chance to express her feelings. Although these original choices (about her education and upbringing) were not directly related to money, she was now using it to express her feelings in the knowledge that had her parents been alive this would have worried them. It became her revenge.

What this illustrated was that Helen's overspending was not just about what she was buying. Almost everyone wants to have luxury and nice things, but not everyone spends more than they can afford to get them.

If you are an overspender then there is always more to the story and this book will help you to get to the root of your emotional spending, so that you can take practical steps towards becoming a reformed overspender.

Can you identify what's going on for you when you are actually there in the moment of spending? Slow down the process to a step-by-step mental exercise. What's really going on as you stand in the queue to pay, as you reach for your wallet, as you hand over the payment, as you receive your goods or services? What are you really feeling moment by moment? Write it down and then think carefully what those feelings remind you of. You might recognise yourself in some of the themes below.

## Overspending themes

We've seen so many different stories and so many reasons for the emotional energy behind destructive spending, but five main themes have emerged and it's worth checking right now to see how vulnerable you might be to them.

### 1. Dads
Do you have unresolved issues with your father, or father figure? Do you punish him financially, or just use money as the only way in which you can communicate with him? Or does the 'male' represent money, institutions and power, and so get up your nose?

Are you punishing yourself in trying to punish your dad?

### 2. The Cinderella complex
Cinderella went from a life of abuse to the life of a princess – rags to riches. And the key moment in her transformation was the granting of the dress for the ball. Many people now take this literally and think that if they could just get the right 'look' their

life would magically improve in every way. It doesn't. Cinderella is an allegory about discovering feminine potential: don't take it too seriously. (See also p. 190.)

### 3. Self-worth

Do you think you are worth much as a person? You might say 'Yes', but if inside you are screaming 'No,' this can be reflected in your finances. Your 'net worth' as a person is the amount of money you have. If your self-worth is much less than your net worth, then you will probably sabotage your finances because you can't believe you deserve them.

### 4. Loss

Every life ends in death. Every relationship ends in sadness. Loss is a fundamental part of life, and yet in our modern culture we often sweep it under the carpet rather than address it in a constructive way. When we can't articulate our distress we often 'act out' how we are feeling. And what better way to try to communicate our despair over loss than to act out a literal loss with money? Throwing your money away can be a cry for help.

### 5. Expensive habits

Sometimes overspenders do not have a problem with money as such, but with something that costs a lot of money – like drugs, for example. The hardest part about getting over such addictions is facing up to them in the first place. Sometimes your finances can provide a big clue as to what else is going wrong in your life, and the need to sort them out can force you to face them head on.

If any of the five themes above rings a bell, then it's definitely time to take stock and prevent further overspending.

# Jay's compulsive spender questionnaire

How many of the answers to the following questions describe your relationship with spending?

- Do you shop almost every day as a way of relieving stress or escaping everyday problems?
- When you are shopping do you experience feelings of euphoria and excitement?
- Do you feel guilty after a big spending trip?
- Do you ever hide your purchases from friends or family?
- Do you buy more than one of the same item and keep things in cupboards or boxes with their price tags on?
- Do you feel stressed about your spending levels?
- Do you use credit crunch or recession as an excuse, i.e. that you need to spend in order to cheer yourself up?
- Do you use your credit cards to fund everyday spending and to take out cash?
- Do you find yourself unable to stop spending on Internet auction sites?
- Do you feel unable to control your spending once you are inside a shop?
- Do you ever stand in a queue to pay and know deep down that you are never going to use the item you are about to buy?
- Do you buy items in bulk so you don't run out?
- Do you move your money around on different cards and accounts kidding yourself that you are in control?
- Do you feel compelled to do Internet shopping every time the computer is on?
- Do you feel pressure to buy to keep up with the latest trends?

- Do you feel huge relief if the cash machine/ATM allows you to take out money?
- Do you shrug off your spending habits as something that everyone does these days?

If you answered 'Yes' to four or more of the above questions, we have some work to do. This step is a wake-up call, many of the things we are asking might be issues you are dealing with for the very first time and this can feel overwhelming. Take your time and follow these steps at a pace that feels right for you.

## Overspending = debt

Overspending – a simple equation of spending more every month than you have coming in – leads to debt, and it's scary just how quickly this can creep up on you. But no one likes to think about debt and it's amazing how easy it is to push it to the back of your mind while you carry on spending.

All of us have a certain amount of debt: mortgages, personal loans, overdrafts, credit cards but it is how you manage these debts that matters. A lot of people have no problems at all with this – they pay their mortgage every month and always pay off their credit card in full. So for them the system works. But for others it is far from ideal and, as the cost of living rises, even sensible spenders can begin to feel the pinch and get into trouble with money.

There are also various stages of life at which your spending can push you out of control leaving you financially stretched. Starting a family, deciding to go back to further education, losing your job, becoming ill or going through a relationship breakdown are all situations that can leave you feeling out of control financially.

Most people tend not to talk openly about money and debt. We've all had drinks with friends and discussed how much our homes are worth, most workers get to know how much colleagues are paid by listening in on office gossip, but if you ask a friend straight up how much debt they are in and how they feel about it you are unlikely to get a straight answer.

In this climate of secrecy it can be easy to think that you might be in the same boat as everyone else, but don't try and cheer yourself up this way. Remember the friend at school who always told you that they, like you, had done no revision for their exams and then when the results came out you realised that their idea of no revision was obviously very different from yours? Don't ever judge your money situation by others' standards as this will only lead to a badly misplaced sense of financial security.

Let's suppose, for example, that a young man becomes involved with a group of people who share an interest in classic cars. Some of them have rare and expensive cars costing them a small fortune in maintenance; but they have money and are able to afford this. When, eventually, the young man begins to feel that he does not really belong in the group as long as he has no decent hardware to show off, he buys a classic car. It's a relatively inexpensive one, but nevertheless beyond his means. He has lost sight of the true context – his own financial picture, as opposed to that of others who are in a different financial league. His emotional need to connect with his 'friends' has driven him to accept a failure in logic, leading him into debt.

# CASE STUDY

Simon put himself about as a successful and dynamic young entrepreneur – young, cocky, full of himself, perhaps slightly annoying, but at the same time somewhat seductive. You could never be sure if you hated him or wanted to be him.

In reality, however, Simon's image was cultivated by spending money he didn't have, and although in a sense all he really wanted was to look rich, in doing so he was making himself poorer and poorer because the things he was spending his money on had no value. His hopes of running a business were being scuppered by bad spending habits.

Simon's particular area of extreme expenditure was what many people may see as a typical male fascination and preoccupation with technology; he was a gadget freak. He had a gadget for everything and he had to have the latest one, to the point of replacing expensive items he had bought just months before.

It took some digging into his past, and his deeper self, to begin to explain this self-destructive behaviour. Simon revealed a very poignant story about his parents' divorce when he was eight years old. He had been aware that things hadn't been going well for some time and there was always a lot of tension at home and perhaps some hostility. But what he remembered very vividly as the first real sign of change – actual physical change – in the family set-up was when his father removed the brand new stereo from the family home. In the miserable phase of his life that followed, somehow the stereo became the key – the thing that signified the passage from one phase of his life to the other.

Simon is a good example of someone who did not realise just how much he needed to get Spendsmart about his money. His obsession with buying all the latest technology was his attempt to buy back the family that he had once had. Once he realised how emotional his spending was, he was able to look at the problem in a different way and, as a bright, capable young man, begin to put practical strategies in place for financial recovery.

# Who is going to fix your debts?

Getting into debt is all too easy to do, but getting out of it takes a lot of hard work and effort to get your money sorted and debts paid back. It is possible to do it, though, and you are not alone – we will take you through the process slowly and systematically, so that you don't feel overwhelmed or confused at any stage.

Whether your money worries are the result of taking on too many loans and running up too many debts, or living above your means from the minute you started earning and never quite catching up, the one thing you need to do now is take responsibility for your overspending. You cannot blame anyone or anything else for your money problems.

We are all bombarded with buy-now-pay-later deals, invitations to apply for shiny new credit cards and sign-up-today offers on store cards. Magazines tell you how to shop and live like your favourite celebrity, your children are always on at you for something new and temptation seems to face us at every turn. But at the end of the day, *you* and *only you* make the choice about what you spend your money on.

You might blame recession, the government, the banks, your friend for egging you on – there will always be a reason to avoid the simple fact that you are in debt because you have put yourself there.

It's tempting to sweep debt under the carpet or to try to justify your spending. You see friends or family buying things that you really want too, which somehow makes spending seem OK. And if you have had a hard week at work and a nasty letter from the bank there is always another credit card you can use for a Saturday spending spree to cheer yourself up.

These days, our sense of entitlement can lead to real problems. We are all victims of the 'because I am worth it' age and we are all guilty of confusing 'want' with 'need'. You pick up a magazine and see Gwyneth Paltrow sporting a pair of Louboutin shoes and you think you should have them too, while a picture of Jude Law in a simple cashmere sweater and a great watch provokes a rush of longing. We all know that feeling.

But the Spendsmart five-step money guide is based on reality, which means getting your head around taking responsibility. Your problems won't be solved by your partner, the credit companies or your parents.

So start by taking stock. Think about debt as something you can deal with. It needs to be in your mind as a reality, not something that is going to be swept under the carpet. Think of it as the enemy and, above all, be bold.

## Debt – the enemy

It is going to take some time and effort to get your money back on track, and there will be moments of despondency, so to keep yourself motivated just focus on the following:

### Having a debt

- Takes away your choices
- Makes life a constant worry
- Reduces your quality of life
- Means you can't think beyond today
- Can affect your relationships if you lie about money
- Makes you feel ashamed and guilty on a day-to-day basis

### Being in credit

- Makes you feel in control
- Stops you feeling overwhelmed and scared
- Opens up possibilities
- Means you are able to plan for your future
- Frees you up from secrets and lies
- Makes you realise you never want to be in debt again

# Working out your total debt today – the easy way

Take a look at the personal debt chart below and either photo-copy it or reproduce it on your computer ready to fill in. Then get all your paperwork together – bills, bank statements, credit card information, letters from agencies – and get to work on the chart. If you don't have everything to hand, call the relevant companies and ask for up-to-date debt figures, but do allow enough time to get all of this done in one go. *Do not* put off making the phone calls and, if necessary, get a friend to come round and keep you going until the whole chart is completed. Once you have done this, add up all the amounts in the first column and you will finally have a figure that is your total debt.

The key to success is to fill it *all* in – don't leave anything out and don't lie to yourself about any of the figures. It is really important to be honest here; it is a very scary thing to do and you have probably been putting it off for months, maybe years, but you *can* do it. And once you have finished you should feel a huge sense of relief.

Don't be alarmed if the total that you owe is more than you'd thought – it's a bit like getting on the scales after Christmas, you know you have overdone it and think you have probably put on four pounds, but the scary reality in January is that all the pre-Christmas partying you had forgotten about, combined with the big event itself, and a New Year blowout has left you a stone fatter than you were before. It is not a nice feeling at all, but comfort yourself with the fact that you now know the worst and we are ready to help you deal with whatever your reality is here.

# THE SPENDSMART PERSONAL DEBT CHART

Fill in the amount of money you owe in each of
the following debt areas.

| DEBT | | AMOUNT OWED | %APR |
|---|---|---|---|
| OVERDRAFT | | | |
| MORTGAGE/RENT ARREARS | | | |
| CAR LOAN | | | |
| CREDIT CARDS | 1 | | |
| | 2 | | |
| | 3 | | |
| STORE CARDS | 1 | | |
| | 2 | | |
| | 3 | | |
| BANK LOAN | | | |
| STUDENT LOAN | | | |
| MONEY OWED TO FRIENDS | | | |
| MONEY OWED TO FAMILY | | | |
| COUNCIL TAX | | | |
| TAX/VAT ARREARS | | | |
| UTILITY BILLS | | | |
| WATER | | | |
| GAS | | | |
| ELECTRICITY | | | |
| MOBILE PHONE | | | |

THE TOTAL AMOUNT OF MY DEBT TODAY IS £

# Sorting out your debts

Now we that we have a figure for your debt, we can begin to move forward. Don't panic – you don't have to do everything at once, but these are the areas you will have to tackle now:

- Talking about your debts
- Looking at your different debts and the available options
- Prioritising your debts and forward planning

You will then need to put together a personal spending chart (see p. 52) to help you identify your specific problem areas.

## Benjamin – talking about your debts

The first step in solving any problem is recognising that there is one. You can't do anything about something if you don't accept its existence. So you can't get Spendsmart unless you are prepared to stand honestly and openly, staring into the abyss of your financial chaos, and take that first brave step away from it, towards a life of calm control. That means counting the problem and making it specific, not just noticing it as a vague issue in general.

Psychologically, truth is a very powerful thing. None of us really knows the truth about anything in its infinite detail. We take life in pieces so that it is more palatable for us. We need our illusions because they make us feel safe and would give them up as reluctantly as we would give up a parachute on falling out of an aeroplane. Psychological safety is our greatest need, but also often our greatest illusion and hang-up.

The Flat Earth Society is a great example of this. Formed in 1547, it was a response to the idea that the earth might be round, a concept in conflict with all sorts of prevailing ideas about the universe on which individuals had founded their own beliefs about themselves and their lives. So when it was suggested that the earth might be round, all hell broke loose. Never mind that someone had actually sailed round the world and proved it; somehow people just didn't feel safe about changing their minds. So they didn't, regardless of the evidence.

Now ask yourself: are you a flat-earther? Are you ignoring the evidence? If so, is that to your advantage? You need to face the reality and be honest with yourself, then you will be able to give yourself some direction.

Now that you have admitted to yourself that you are in trouble, and that you are going to change, you need to share this news with your partner, your friends and your family. People often fear being judged by others according to their bank balance, which can make talking about money and debt quite difficult. But once they start talking, most people find that having a support system really makes a difference and that the majority of friends or family are more than willing to help them work towards a solution.

It is essential that you tell your partner if you have been keeping money secrets from them. In practical terms, if they don't know about the situation they may continue to spend and plan causing further problems. Plus, if you have joint financial agreements they may be liable for your debt if you default. On an emotional level, it may lead to a serious breakdown in trust if they find out the truth from someone other than you.

Talk about it right now as it gets harder the longer you wait. Don't joke about your debt or shrug it off – tell your partner how it makes you feel and explain that you will need their emotional support while you sort it all out.

Relationship experts say that money issues are responsible for a huge percentage of the problems that couples present with. Money is a bigger issue than sex and is cited as the cause of more arguments than are issues relating to family or friends. It is, therefore, vital that all money problems are aired so that they can be addressed in a positive and productive way.

## Looking at your different debts and the available options

### Your bank account

Most people open a bank account when they are a student or have just started work. You may have been lured in with offers of gift vouchers, free CDs and probably some good deals that worked for you. Or at least they might have been good deals then, but they are probably not so good for your situation now.

Few people change their bank account, which makes no sense at all when you realise that the banks are well aware of this and are in no hurry to inform you of better deals. Your ignorance is their bliss, so it's up to you to take responsibility when it comes to your bank account and sort it out for yourself. Here are some tips on what to look for:

- Never pay for a current account and make sure you check what is around on the money comparison sites.
- The banks really want new current account clients so you may find deals that offer a cash incentive. Check out the deal if this is the case.
- Some online banks offer interest on current accounts but in your position you should be searching out the bank with the best overdraft offers and rates.

- Remember, every bank will charge you if you go over your authorised overdraft limit and these costs can mount up fast.

If you are stuck with your current bank, then check out what they have on offer – they may well have a lot of accounts that will give you a significantly better deal. You should call the bank or go in to see them; doing things online does not help in this instance. Talking to your bank about the fact that you recognise you are in trouble means they will take you seriously and should be quite helpful. Tell them that you are in the process of working out a new budget for yourself and that you will send a copy to them when you have finalised it, within the next month.

Things you should ask when you visit your bank are:

- Can they offer you a better deal than the one you are getting?
- Can they stop the charges and interest on your account so that the amount you pay them back starts to reduce your debt immediately?
- If they are unable to authorise this, can they give you the regional or head office number so that you can speak to someone who can?
- Can they explain to you what the interest rates would be if you wanted to consolidate your debts and take out one bigger loan with them?
- Can they explain their redemption penalties – i.e. if you suddenly got a lump sum from an inheritance or a bonus could you pay your loan back quicker without being penalised?
- Do they offer a service whereby they send you a text message when you are about to reach your limit?

Take this book with you and don't be intimidated. It's in their interest that you stay solvent (able to pay) and that you repay your debts rather than having to declare yourself bankrupt or go under, as that would mean them having to take you to court to recover their money. Also, feel free to remind them that the banking code states banks 'will consider cases of financial difficulty sympathetically and positively' and point out you are doing your bit and trying to be responsible.

## What are unauthorised bank charges?

There has been quite a lot of publicity about people fighting back and claiming what they consider to have been unfair charges. It is a bit of a grey area, but you can get up-to-date information on this and on what to do if you feel that your bank has charged you unfairly by logging on to the sites listed on p. 223.

## Interest charges

Your debts will comprise two parts:

1) the money that you have borrowed (or spent on a card)
2) the interest that is added to that debt, i.e. what you are charged for the loan of that money.

If you have a fixed-term loan, the interest on your debt was worked out at the start of your agreement and is included in your monthly payments. If you miss a payment on a loan like this, the creditor might charge you a penalty for something they call 'default' interest.

## Credit and store card debts

You need to ask your creditors to freeze all the interest they are adding on to your accounts. If you have any fixed-term loans outstanding, do ask your creditors to freeze any default interest they are currently adding to your debt as that will help.

Use the template letter below to get your creditors to freeze your account as soon as possible. This will show your creditors that you are taking your problems seriously, and most should be accommodating. If they refuse your request then the National Debt Helpline and Consumer Credit Counselling services (see p. 224) can give you more information and help with your particular circumstances.

Any company you write to will expect you to follow through with your promise to get back to them within twenty-eight days with an offer of payment. The reason why you cannot make an offer at this stage is because we have not worked out your final budget yet (this will be done in Step Four); you still need to send these letters out now though, in order to halt your debts and prevent them from getting any bigger. You can then use the twenty-eight days' grace to do all you can to help yourself, so that when you do write back to them with an offer it is one that is sustainable in the long term.

---

### SPENDSMART TEMPLATE FOR LETTER REQUESTING AN INTEREST FREEZE ON YOUR ACCOUNT/LOAN

Dear Sir/Madam

**Re: credit card no./loan ref.**

I am writing to inform you that I am in financial difficulty and am in the process of getting assistance to sort out the problems I am experiencing.

I would ask that you hold any action on the above account for a period of twenty-eight days. Could you please freeze the interest and/or any other charges accruing and I will get back to you within the stated time with an offer of payment.

I look forward to hearing from you.

Yours faithfully

---

### Switch your credit card debt and get a better deal

One thing you can do with your credit card debt is to switch the amount you owe to another credit card.

Ideally, you would transfer your debt onto a card that has a 0 per cent balance transfer, and make sure that you go for the one with the longest fee-free term you can find. This means your debt will be transferred onto a card that charges no interest and you then get to pay back your debt at 0 per cent. However, there is a huge number of cards out there, so you will need to do some research to find those with the best deals.

The next-best alternative is to pay a fee – usually around a 2 per cent charge – and switch to a card that offers something called a life of balance transfer. This is where you pay your debt off on the new card at the rate of interest they charge (usually really low) and not the high rate on your existing card.

Be aware that you should only do these transfers if you *never* use the new card to make purchases. You need to view it as an interest-free loan option, not as a new credit card. If you put your debt on this new card, then use it for a spending spree, you will end up worse off than ever before. Read the small print though, to make sure that you are not charged for non-use of the card and be aware of the company's terms before you sign up. Don't be afraid to call the company and ask them as many questions as you like.

The other reason why you should not use your new card is that some companies make you pay your new debt off last. That would mean you having to repay the debt you transferred to them first, and in the meantime you'd be charged a huge interest rate on the new debt. It's too easy to end up owing enormous sums on credit cards for what seemed like a small purchase at the time.

It cannot be stressed enough how dangerous it is to run up more debt on these cards. If you are in any doubt as to whether you would have the discipline to cut up these cards once you have used them for a credit transfer, don't even consider it as an option.

## Never use your credit card for cash

Never be tempted to take out cash on your credit cards. What none of the companies tells you is that any cash you withdraw starts piling up a debt at a huge rate the minute you make a withdrawal. If you repay the minimum every month it can take years to clear the debt, plus you will end up having paid back considerably more than you withdrew in the first place. Hardly a good offer.

---

## Debt-free management plans (DMP)

With a DMP you make one payment every month to cover all your credit card debts and this will be divided up and sent to your creditors every month for you by the National Debt Helpline. They can set you up with a DMP plan for free, but to be eligible for help you have to owe above a certain amount on three or more credit cards. This option means that you don't have to negotiate directly with your creditors to accept your offer and it freezes the interest on your credit card debts fast.

---

## Charge cards

Charge cards differ from credit cards in that you have to pay the full balance off each month and they will have high APR rates (annual percentage rate). It can be harder to negotiate reduced offers of payment with these companies and they can take legal action to recover their debts. The National Debt Helpline will have up-to-date information on the best thing to do with regard to your own particular charge card/s.

## Student loans

Most students leave full-time education with a hefty debt comprised of bank overdraft fees, credit card debts and bank loans. This needs to be sorted out fast. The bank overdraft will probably have been interest free but unless you move it into a graduate account when you leave university you will be charged interest.

All the banks offer graduate accounts and allow you to transfer your high-rate borrowing into lower-rate accounts once you leave university. Don't be tempted by free gifts when you sign up for a graduate account – focus on the best offers in terms of interest rates as you may be paying off these debts for quite some time.

There are students who think that they can rack up huge debts while at university, then declare themselves bankrupt when they graduate so that they don't have to repay their student loan and card debts. This is extremely foolhardy and the government has now excluded student debts from bankruptcy regulations. The most sensible course is to get a job during the holidays and keep your loan to a minimum. Some students who do this actually finish university with zero debts!

## Mortgages

Check that your mortgage is still competitive and, if not, move it now if you can. Most mortgage companies will make you pay a deeds release fee and some charge an arrangement fee if you want to move. But most now waive the fees for solicitors and valuations so that you only have to pay an arrangement fee, which can be added on to your new mortgage.

Falling behind with mortgage payments is serious. Do not ignore letters from the mortgage company and check your agreement to see if your loan is unsecured or secured. If it is a secured loan then call them straight away and tell them you are in difficulty and will get back to them within twenty-eight days with a repayment plan (we are going to work this out in Step Four).

If you have not paid your mortgage for a couple of months start paying now – even if you do not pay the full amount it still makes a difference and reduces the chances of the mortgage company taking action against you.

One option your lender might offer is to add your payment arrears to your total mortgage (known as capitalising the arrears) and increase your monthly payments to take this into account. You are more likely to be given this option if you have kept to a payment agreement for some months because it shows you are serious about getting things back on track.

If you have an endowment mortgage you may be able to change to a repayment one. Your endowment mortgage will have included an insurance policy and if you have had this for a few years it may have a value if you surrender it. However, if you are considering this option, don't just listen to your mortgage company about whether it is worth doing – get some independent financial advice before you do anything.

Another alternative worth investigating is increasing your mortgage term. The usual term is twenty-five years, so you could ask your lender to extend it back to the original twenty-five or even thirty years, depending on how long you have had your mortgage for.

If you have a repayment mortgage, you might consider switching to an interest-only plan. This need only be a short-term measure, just until you've repaid your debts.

Should you want to speak to someone about all the options, check out independent financial advisers near you. You can either pay a flat fee to an adviser for their time and advice, or pay nothing and the adviser will take their commission from the company whose product they recommend (this may mean, however, that they are not impartial).

## Rent arrears to council or housing associations

If you are in arrears with your rent and are a council or housing association tenant then your landlord is obliged to follow strict guidelines. They must contact you to try and agree what you should pay towards your rent arrears. They must also arrange for your rent to be paid through direct payments if you are on benefits and help you with any claim you have for housing benefit. They should not take possession action if you keep up with an agreement to pay your rent and something towards your arrears.

## Owing rent to a private landlord

Your contract will probably be an assured shorthold tenancy and you should contact the landlord or the management company that act for them as soon as possible if you are experiencing financial difficulty. Your landlord can take court action if you have rent arrears of more than eight weeks or if you have consistently delayed in paying your rent.

Keep paying as much as you can and try to reach an agreement before your landlord sends you a notice of possession proceedings. If you have already been served with one, contact the National Debt Helpline for legal advice.

## Debts on hire purchase (HP)

Do prioritise this debt as it can be an expensive loan and, if you don't keep up payments, you could end up losing both the goods and the money you have already paid out.

Most people take out an HP agreement when they buy a car or goods for their home. You pay a deposit and then agree to make the rest of the payments in monthly instalments. The agreement states that until you have paid the whole debt off, the goods in question are actually owned by the company you bought them from, i.e. your creditor. If, for any reason, you stop paying, the goods can be repossessed, and if you have paid less than a third of the total amount you can be taken to court for the balance of payment. If, however, you have paid more than a third of the total amount owing, the goods cannot be claimed by the creditor without them going through the county court. The creditors do need a court order if they want to remove goods from your home but if the goods are in a public place, for example a car on a public road, they can be reclaimed at any time.

If the creditor has applied to reclaim goods, the court will have sent you a claim form. This gives you the chance to return the goods yourself and also to fill in an admission form, informing them of your financial situation and allowing you to make a new offer of monthly payments.

If you want to end the HP agreement by handing back the goods, you can, but the creditors may ask for up to half the total figure of the original amount less what you have already paid, regardless of when you end it. You will also have to pay the arrears and a sum for wear and tear on the goods.

## Debts with catalogue companies

Once you have received goods from a catalogue company they belong to you and cannot be taken away if you do not pay.

Debts with a catalogue company should be treated in the same way as credit card debts. Most catalogues operate on monthly payments, so you explain your situation to them using the template letter on p. 36. It's also a good idea to ask them to stop sending you any new catalogues so that you will not be tempted to make new purchases while you are paying off your debt.

## Collection agencies

Your creditors may have passed your debt on to a collection agency, especially if you have not been answering letters or final demands. Don't panic if you open a letter from one of these – they are not bailiffs and they have no right to enter your home and seize any of your goods. Negotiate with them in the same way as you do other creditors but do be aware that they may be entitled to charge you extra fees if they have to come and collect the money you owe from your home.

## Debts to family and friends

Just because it was your mum or your best friend that lent you some money and not a bank, this is still a debt, only it has emotional involvement attached. Make regular monthly offers of payment that will probably be totally interest free unless the friend or family member in question is really sick of you.

It is completely unacceptable to accept loans from family and friends and not pay them back, no matter how broke you are or how wealthy they may be. The reality is that they care about you and did something generous to help you out. They deserve to be treated with the utmost respect.

Even if they say they don't want the money back, you should insist that you are going to repay it as it would make you feel better, and tell them you would appreciate their help by letting you pay an agreed amount every month until you are clear from the debt. Otherwise there is a real danger here of setting up an unhealthy culture around money, debt and repayment.

Dismissing personal debts is a definite sign that there is a problem of accountability and you should not underestimate the importance of facing up to dealing with this. Every debt recovery success story we have come across has involved

43

people who have paid back friends and family and felt better for it. Those who write off these debts as trivial tend to end up back where they started, expecting someone else to dig them out of ever-deepening debt holes. Make sure that this is not you.

## CASE STUDY

Anna started getting into debt relatively innocuously with a loan from her mother to help with the cost of doing up her first home. However, there were some unresolved issues in their relationship stemming from Anna's resentment of her mother's behaviour at the time of her parents' divorce, added to which family tensions were running high with Anna's father having recently died following a long illness. So in a way, the money was more than just cash; it was a way for Anna's mother to try to comfort her daughter.

Because neither of them had any practical discipline over what was essentially an emotional transaction, things spiralled out of control. Anna ended up owing her mother an enormous sum and when her mother was no longer able to help her, Anna went on to run up huge commercial debts. The amount Anna owed her mother was double what she was earning after tax and repaying the loan seemed a hopeless case.

However, once she had spoken up to her mother about her true feelings about the divorce, Anna was able to approach her mum with renewed confidence in herself. She set up a standing order to repay the money in small weekly instalments and stuck to it. Although the payments did not constitute a huge financial return for her mother, it allowed both of them to feel much better about the situation, and thus repair their relationship and take away some of the reasons for Anna's spending in the first place.

## Consolidating your debts

Debt consolidation can really simplify things for you by putting all your debts into one big account so that you make just one payment a month to pay it all off. All banks and building societies offer personal loans enabling you to do this and now that you know your total debt you can shop around and compare the rates that are on offer.

Never be tempted to apply for help to companies that advertise on TV or in the media. They *will* consolidate your loan and give you a low interest rate, but the repayment period will be so long that you'll end up paying them a scary sum. They can also make you sign a form saying that your debt is secured against your home (if you own one); this means that if you default on your monthly payment they can come after your home.

The only people to get impartial advice from are the National Debt Helpline and the Consumer Credit Counselling Service (see p. 224).

## Lump-sum payments to creditors

You can offer your creditors a lump sum to settle your debts even if the amount you are offering is less than the total amount you owe. Most people get the lump sum by remortgaging their home. Creditors are under no obligation to accept a sum in full and final settlement of your debt, but if your circumstances look unlikely to improve they may agree.

If you feel that you are in a position to do this you should get further advice from the National Debtline or the Consumer Credit Counselling Service, as they are experts in lump-sum payment offers.

## Can I declare myself bankrupt?

Since 2004 it has been much easier to declare yourself bankrupt, and some people now view it as a good way to get their debts written off and start over. Opting for bankruptcy, however, is not easy.

Once you declare yourself bankrupt (your creditors are unlikely to make you bankrupt), you don't own anything and your possessions become the property of the official receiver who will sell them. This will involve a stranger coming to your house, going through your wardrobe, your kitchen, your CD collection, and taking anything they think is worth selling. You can say goodbye to your TV, computer, designer handbags, expensive jeans and obviously your home if you own one.

While you are bankrupt you will not have a bank account, mobile phone account (apart from a pay-as-you-go account), credit cards, or be able to rent a property, get a mortgage or sign on for utilities such as gas and electricity. The fact that you are bankrupt will also be announced in the paper. You may lose your job (check your contract of employment as most companies now have a clause stating that they are not responsible for keeping bankrupts on), and, if you work in finance, or are a solicitor or accountant, you will get struck off.

You will find it extremely difficult to ever get any kind of credit in the future; you'll be listed with the credit agencies for six years, after which – if you do manage to persuade any company to give you credit – you will be charged at a much higher rate than other people. If you are eventually approved for a mortgage you will be paying around 2 per cent more than others, which can add up to a lot of money.

So while you may feel that bankruptcy today has no stigma attached to it, don't assume that other people and organisations share your view. They don't.

## An individual voluntary arrangement

This is a formal arrangement you can take out through the county court. It usually requires you to pay an agreed amount towards your debts over five years. The IVA, as it is known, will be set up and managed by an insolvency practitioner who is responsible for paying your money out to the credit card companies and banks to whom you owe money.

In order for your practitioner to arrange an IVA they need at least 75 per cent of your creditors to agree to it, and at the end of the five-year period you are declared clear, even if you have not paid off all your original debts.

The advantage to this system is that you are seen to be making an effort to take responsibility for your debts, and you get to keep all of your belongings. The disadvantage is that insolvency practitioners are expensive, as they know you need their services. They charge a set fee to act on your behalf in addition to a monthly charge. This means less money each month going to pay off your debts. You need to be careful if you own your home as you can risk losing it if you don't keep up all your payments.

## Your credit rating explained

You are entitled to see a copy of your credit report (this is held by the main credit reference agencies). Arrears of payments show up for thirty-six months but defaulted accounts such as county court judgments stay on your record for six years. Your records will also show when you have paid off your debts.

If you are refused credit you have the right to ask which credit reference agency has been approached and you can apply to know why that company has turned you down. They should tell you if they used a credit scoring system. You can either write to the main agencies enclosing a small fee and they should send you all the information within seven days, or you can download your details. If any information is wrong you have the right to change it. If you have paid your debts and that has not been noted you can ask them to mark your file as 'satisfied' to show that this has been done.

You can improve your credit rating by not applying for any more credit. Each time you apply it leaves what is known as a 'footprint' and too many of these can lower your score, especially if you are consistently rejected.

# Prioritising your debts and forward planning

We've looked at all the different types of debt, now we need to prioritise them.

## Not all debts are the same

You know exactly what your debts are now, as you have completed a personal debt chart (see p. 29). This may well make you feel that you want to sort out a payment plan immediately and get the debts sorted. But this is not the right time to rush into doing a budget plan that will be unsustainable and based on panic. What you need to do next is to decide who is going to get paid back first.

At the front of the queue are those creditors charging you the highest APR percentage. These will probably be any store cards you have and some credit cards. Putting debts in an order like this will make it easy for you to see which company or card is making you pay back the most in interest, and these are the debts you need to sort out first. Student loans and loans from family and friends will therefore fall to the bottom of your pay-back list but must not be ignored.

People who get into trouble with money often resort to short-term fixes with loans from well-meaning family and friends, which then become long-term, informal loans from people who become less well meaning. Typically, these loans carry no interest or penalties, but that's only on the surface.

Losing face with family and friends and sliding down the slippery slope of financial incompetence in front of your nearest and dearest can have a hidden inner cost. Your self-esteem can suffer when you see your worst fears about yourself reflected in the eyes of those who care for you. This can become shameful and unbearable, and, often, the response to these feelings is to spend for momentary relief. But of course, all you are doing is reinforcing the perception that you can't cope, and making things financially more difficult for yourself.

The upside of settling things with family and friends is that, if you are honest, you will get a more human reception than from a bank. If you are truthful about how difficult you are finding things, they will respect your honesty and you will regain their trust. This, coupled with your new self-knowledge, can become the springboard for making proper, formal arrangements about debts with family and friends, which actually may help you to grow both financially and personally as you settle them. You will get better terms for your debt than a store card, but you'll also restore your own confidence in managing your relationships, both with money and people, which in turn will make you less likely to need emotional spending to cope.

So, financially speaking, you need to start paying the highest interest rate loans off first, but emotionally speaking you need to face up to and address the ones that have the most personal involvement. This might mean paying your credit cards as a priority while agreeing a much lower schedule of payments with friends and family until the former is under control, and making sure that you stick to both plans religiously.

## Fill in a personal spending list

Taking time to get used to the reality of knowing what your debt is and understanding how and why you are going to pay it back is important. And, as we have already said, it is equally crucial to the success of this plan that you follow the steps in order. In Step Four you will work out your new budget and repayment scheme. The reason we are not going to do it now is that you need to work through Steps Two and Three first to understand how you got to this point, so that you can understand and collect the vital personal information you will need to ensure that the final budget is realistic for your situation, as you may be on it for a very long time.

Photocopy the list below (or, as before, reproduce it on your computer), adding or deleting categories depending on your circumstances. The reason why you need to fill this in now is because it will alert you to areas in which you may still be overspending or wasting money and there's no reason why you shouldn't start working on that now. Once you have completed the chart and highlighted any areas in which you need to cut back, put it away somewhere safe until we get to Step Four.

---

## Why there is never *more* money in the bank than we think!

It appears that there's not a single person alive who would estimate their spending at more than it actually is. We all seem constantly amazed by how much less money we have in the bank than we'd anticipated. Why is that?

A computer will work sequentially – each piece of data and detail being as important as the next – and it will just plough through it all from start to finish. We, however, will start with an overview, a snapshot that allows us to gain an instant approximation of an under-standing of the whole; this is useful to us in making judgments and decisions. However, as we make these guestimates, we lose data; we give up on those little bits of information that don't inform our global view. Unfortunately, a bank statement is produced by a computer and not by a person expressing an opinion. That's why we don't get on with them too well!

---

## Moving ahead

Remember – knowledge is power. And the reasons for which you are reading this book mean that power is one thing you are running out of – the power to spend without thinking twice about it. So we need to empower you in another way. Aristotle said, 'Know thyself,' by which he meant that with self-knowledge all things become possible. Once you know who you really are, then you know your limits and what you can do. Thus, paradoxically, all things become possible, because in knowing

# THE SPENDSMART PERSONAL SPENDING CHART

Fill in your approximate monthly spend on each item.

| ITEM | APPROXIMATE SPEND |
|---|---|
| Mortgage or rent | |
| Household insurance | |
| Gas and/or electricity | |
| Water bill | |
| Home phone bill | |
| Mobile phone bill | |
| Internet bill | |
| TV licence | |
| Sky/Virgin | |
| Council tax | |
| Car Insurance | |
| Petrol | |
| Car tax | |
| AA/RAC or similar | |
| Taxis | |
| Train fares | |
| Any things like private healthcare, travel insurance, British Gas cover plan | |
| Pet insurance | |
| Supermarket shopping | |
| Work lunches | |
| Eating out | |
| Drinks out | |
| Clothes | |
| Toiletries | |
| Beauty treatments/haircuts | |
| Newspapers and magazines | |
| Snacks and coffee break items | |
| Children outgoings eg. childcare, babysitting, clothes, nappies, etc | |
| Gym memberships | |
| Sports and hobbies | |
| Holidays and weekend breaks | |

THE TOTAL I HAVE BEEN SPENDING IN AN AVERAGE MONTH IS £

THE TOTAL I EARN IN AN AVERAGE MONTH IS £

MY OVERSPEND EVERY MONTH IS £

your limits you remove them; you are able to make sensible plans based on what you can and cannot do yourself.

This principle can be applied to money. Anything is possible as long as you have the courage to look honestly and dispassionately at yourself, assess the scale of the problem with which you are confronted and work sensibly towards solving it. It's all too easy to look at the tasks in this book and shrug them off saying that you 'can't' do them, or they're 'too hard', or 'not your thing'. It takes courage to change, and a lot of hard work, but there is nothing in this book that you can't do. None of it requires any expertise. If you can use a phone, a pen and a calculator, then you can do it all.

## Spendsmart reality – summary

You might be finding that this start to sorting out your money is overwhelming. Of course it is! Otherwise it would be easy and you'd have done it all by now without ever needing this book.

The way the human brain works is that we are really scared of things we don't understand, while we can work quite confidently with things that we do. Take magic, for example: there is something quite unsettling, even frightening, about watching a magician at work, doing something that is seemingly unexplained, and you may spontaneously recoil from it; once the trick is explained to you, however, you find that you can watch it again without feeling uneasy at all.

So it is with the magic trick that is your disappearing cash. Only in this case, Spendsmart is the explanation – use it to rid yourself of all of your fears and anxieties.

Acknowledging a problem when you neither understand it nor know what to do about it is just plain terrifying. But on the other hand, it's really hard to know what to do about a problem unless you actually admit that it's there. With Spendsmart reality you will have laid the foundations for what follows. You should, by now, have gained a full understanding of yourself and your situation. Make sure you haven't skipped over anything or been dishonest; don't cheat yourself before you've even begun.

If you have been thinking that you'll just read the book first then do the 'reality' later, you're probably avoiding something. And that something is likely to be the one thing that's really undermining your efforts to get your money straightened out. So right here, right now, before you move on to Step Two, write down what it is that you are hoping to avoid dealing with. Find the courage to look honestly at who you are and what you've got to do. Then we'll continue to discover how to do it together.

STEP **2** TWO

# Spendsmart Preparation

## Taking back control

Step Two of Spendsmart will give you the tools to plan a future in which you feel in control. Having discovered the 'reality' in Step One, we will now deal with clearing a space – both mental and physical – in your life.

As knowledge of the extent of your debt and overspending sinks in, you will probably begin to feel extremely uncomfortable. The realisation that the price of living like a celebrity for the last five years is going to take you a long time to pay off is not fun. However, money is freedom in life, and that's what you need to concentrate on, as paying back your debts is going to give you the freedom to face your future with confidence.

Control is a big part of what we fantasise about when we think of having money. Rich people seem to be able to do whatever they want; the world works for them, not the other way around. But control can also be a state of mind and an attitude. It costs you nothing to decide to take control and you don't have to be rich to be determined.

## Benjamin – getting your support system in place

Something you are going to need as you work through this process is a support system. This could be someone you know – friends, family – or a debt support group or counsellor. But you are going to need something or, more accurately, someone.

As a species we work better in groups. We have adapted to be able to function on a deep biological level as inter-related individuals in small societies. So small teams get more done than the same number of individuals working independently.

One of the key safety nets that a group provides for us is the curative option of talking through our problems. Talking, interacting, laughing, crying, sharing – these all contribute to the routine maintenance of our highly sophisticated brain and nervous system. When we try to get by without them we really struggle.

So talking to someone about what's going on will inevitably become important eventually, if it hasn't already. You need to externalise the dialogue that might be going on in your head. Saying the words out loud to another person is a different process and, as such, it affects you in a different way. People often report not having realised that they would feel happy/sad/angry about something that has been going round and round their head until they articulated it. This happens because they are moving the thought out of themselves, and, in so doing, they are allowing an emotion to begin. E-motion means moving out. When the words move out of your head, the feelings can also move out of your heart. Both are important and both are good for you.

The other upside to sharing your situation and reality with others is that you can ask for their help; in fact you might find that they spontaneously offer it! No one can help you if they don't know what's going on. And while this may sound like the opposite of what you want, it just may be exactly what you need.

The fear of letting other people get to know who you really are, what you really do, and how you really think, and particularly of needing their help, can be a sign that you were let down in the past by people that you relied upon. For many of us this is our parents or parental substitutes, since they are the first people that we rely on in our lives. The problem is that this sets up in us a terrible trap. As children, if we were in a situation which felt overwhelming, we often had no way to escape it because we had no independence or resources, so our only way out would have been through some mental agility: we would have convinced ourselves that we were OK and didn't need any help, and that way make everything all right and everybody good enough. This is a good survival strategy, but we have to remember to drop it in later life. Otherwise, as adults, we end up believing that we don't need anything from anyone and that we can sort out our problems on our own. Sound familiar?

With your money issues you could use all the emotional and practical support you can get. It will keep you encouraged, safe and informed. If you've never told anyone about your money worries, then pick up the phone right now and tell one person. You'll be amazed at the difference it makes.

## Jay – sort out your space

It may seem odd that a really vital part of Spendsmart's Step Two is getting your living space under control. However, it is very important when you feel out of control in one area, i.e. spending money, that you feel able to control another area – your home.

Overspenders tend to overspend in all areas, and it's easy to predict that you have probably accumulated a great deal of 'stuff'. Being surrounded by things that you cannot manage can make you feel miserable and also tie you to the past by reminding you of your overspending habits. You find yourself with huge amounts of things that you have struggled to pay for that worry you, nag at your conscience and depress you. We need to create a place where you feel safe and secure, not emotionally and literally overwhelmed.

## Spendsmart Step Two plan of action

The action plan for Step Two is to:

- Clear out your living space – learn to let go and free yourself from all your unnecessary purchases.
- Look at how you live – remember what you have learned about your overspending in Step One and identify your common spending areas.
- Become a seller not a buyer.
- Look at where you could be wasting money and stop.

# CASE STUDY

Jeremy was a typical bloke in his twenties. His flat was so messy it looked as though it had been hit by an earthquake and everything else in his life was the same: his relationships were a bit of a mess, he was rarely on time, he couldn't hold down a job, his spending was all out of control. Yet somehow you could forgive all of this because of his charming personality. Everyone liked him. So what was really going on with him?

One of the first challenges that Jeremy faced when he decided it was time to sort out his money was to literally clear up his mess. The problem was that every time Jeremy sorted out an area of his physical life, he found that he was struggling to cope with what it unearthed. When he cleared his bedroom, he realised that he was lonely and had few possessions that he really cared about. It had been easier when everything was a mess and he didn't have to see what was really there, or more to the point, not there.

So mess can be something we use as a screen to shield us from having to see what's there. If you want to get to the bottom of what's holding you back, you'll need to get clarity on who you are and how you are living. Only then, when you see what you don't like about it, can you do something to focus on either changing it, or understanding why you are so reluctant to recognise it.

When Jeremy took a close look at his history, he found that as a child of a soldier, he had moved often and didn't like it, so he held on to his 'stuff' almost as an armour against this fragmenting experience. It wasn't until Jeremy found the courage as an adult to open up to the idea of what he'd lost as a child from this experience that he began to see that the 'stuff' was now just getting in the way, rather than keeping him safe.

## Benjamin – clearing out and letting go

We can all be resistant to change sometimes, in particular when it applies to our 'stuff'. You see it in young children who become irrationally attached to a security object, such as a blanket or a teddy; even though their chosen object is disgusting and there are much nicer ones available the child would not swap it for the world, and becomes highly distressed without it. Why?

We somehow seem to invest in objects a certain amount of security. We become used to things, and seeing that they remain unchanged helps us to feel safe in some important way. But is this just another way of fooling ourselves that we have some control over the ultimate truth of life; that the one thing that never changes is change itself?

As you will have noticed when you look at the mess that accumulates around your house, the universe gravitates towards chaos rather than order. So control over our lives is something we have to struggle for, rather than something that happens easily. Although we will never have life fully under control, making an effort to control what we can seems really important to us and gives us a vital sense of security. This might be an illusion, but it makes our lives more manageable from day to day. That's why often keeping things the same makes us feel calmer than constant changes.

This is not necessarily a bad thing. If we are settled, we can be productive. And while most things are not changing we can focus on making changes that we do actually want to happen. So sometimes, getting rid of the background to our lives at a time when other changes are already slightly overwhelming can seem illogical. But the background to your life is sometimes also a symptom of the foreground problem. If you were Spendsmart already then the stuff that surrounds you would look different. There would be less of it. It would be more useful. It would suit you better. So getting rid of things that are a product of not being Spendsmart is a step towards the control you want, not away from it.

There's no way to remove from the human psyche the desire to leave things the way they are. You just have to recognise it, acknowledge that it's not helpful and take a deep breath before weighing in with the bin bags. You'll get where you want to be much quicker if you're prepared to start with a blank canvas rather than painting over whatever is already filling the frame.

You might also be able to gain some perspective on why you clutter your life with material goods by going into a high street shop and not buying anything at all. Then see how this leaves you feeling, and talk to someone about it. This is the way forward if you find yourself unable to give up 'stuff' (see Kerry's story, p. 61 for more insight on this).

## Jay – look at how you live

You need to know what it feels like to be unburdened, to have proper space and order in your home, to feel in control. This doesn't mean having to adopt some sort of crazy minimalist lifestyle, it just means having a clean, organised space where you can sit quietly and calmly to make some pretty big decisions about your future.

Your home should be a safe base, where you belong, where you feel secure. But for many overspenders it is not, which helps to explain why they go out so much – they can't face the reality of their living space as it's a constant reminder of their overspending. It's also too chaotic to relax in and too much of a dump to ever invite people over.

So be honest and answer these questions:

- Do you have cupboards overflowing with food?
- Are your fridge and freezer jammed full?
- Do you have too many DVDs, CDs and videos for your shelf space?
- Are your children's bedrooms full of toys they don't play with?
- Is your wardrobe crammed with clothes you never wear?
- Do you have items that are still in their boxes or still have labels on?
- Is your bathroom full of half-used products and lotions?
- Do you have a shed crammed with barbecues and unused garden gear?
- Do you have to park your car outside your home as your garage is full of DIY tools, unused gym equipment, old computer gear or a broken TV?

If you have answered 'Yes' to most of the above, here's what to do – and what not to do – next.

- **DO** designate one room at a time to clear out.
- **DO** create two piles – one for charity shops and one for things you could resell.
- **DON'T** just move stuff around and put it back – be honest and ruthless about things that need to go.
- **DO** ask a friend to come over and help you.
- **DO** put enough time aside to do the job properly.
- **DO** be prepared to feel emotional while you are working through this exercise.

This exercise has been done many times by many people and a lot of them have made a significant amount of money out of it. And it stands to reason – the bigger your debt, the more things you should have lying around to help you out!

---

## What is worth selling?

You can expect to be able to sell any of the following: unopened CDs and DVDs; books; children's toys; Nintendos, PlayStations and games; computers, cameras and printers; kitchen equipment; items you bought for hobbies you never took up; gym equipment; and unused furniture.

In addition lots of websites nowadays make it easy to shift your second-hand clothes if they are newish and designer. Also, mobile phone equipment can get you cash back. The Directory lists websites you can visit where you type in the model you have and they will tell you how much it is worth. Some even send you a postage-paid envelope to put it in. They then recycle your old phone and you get a cheque.

---

## Be ruthless with your wardrobe

One of the hardest things to do is getting people to part with their clothes, as many feel that their wardrobe represents an emotional investment and is part of their identity. Your wardrobe can also be a really telling place, giving you some insight into where a lot of your money has been going.

Start by taking everything out of your wardrobe and piling it on the bed. Beware of your instincts at this point – you will want to find reasons to keep things, but you need to focus on selling stuff that you simply do not need.

## Unworn clothes

Any item that still has the price tag on is going to be sold. Also going are any items you bought in several colours – chances are you've worn the black one but have never quite got round to tearing the tags off the grey, blue, green and red ones you bought at the same time.

## Designer labels

Jeans, jackets, shoes anything that has a designer label should be viewed as a potential money-spinner for resale. Some designers hold their value more than others but people will pay for quality, just as you did, the difference being that you could not afford it.

## Former work clothes

If you have work clothes such as suits that you used to wear to the office, but your job or lifestyle has changed and made them redundant, then shift them. Just keep one favourite interview outfit and that is it.

## Celebrity clothes

This sort of stuff would be great if you lived the lifestyle of Brad and Angelina, but the reality is that you spend Friday nights in the pub and not on the red carpet. Don't resist selling these clothes because you feel bad about what you paid for them. After all, every time you open your wardrobe and see them still in there it makes you feel bad, so better to say goodbye and hope they raise you some cash.

## Fantasy clothes

Get rid of any clothes that don't fit you because you have either lost or put on weight. Try things on and if they do not fit you *today* they are going.

### Emotional clothes

Do not hang on to any clothes that are unwearable just because they remind you of an ex-lover, a particular time in your life or were bought by someone special. There are plenty of other ways to remember people or times, so don't clog up your wardrobe with nostalgic old favourites.

Whatever is left after all this needs to be hung up so that you can see what you have got. Store summer clothes in vacuum bags during winter and vice versa so that you don't have to battle an overstuffed wardrobe every morning.

Once you have done the wardrobe then get going with the same principles on other rooms in the house. Clear outdated stuff from the bathroom, and unused toys and outgrown clothes from the children's room; declutter the garage so you can actually get back in it and get sorting all those hundreds of CDs and clutter in the living room. Do a room a day and don't get overwhelmed or give up. It's worth it: just imagine how much every item on the selling pile is going to get you and that should help you to focus.

## Benjamin – why we should all embrace swapping

Swapping is a great way of connecting with the society around you rather than carrying on the typical economic cycle of individual competition. Everyone has stuff in their life that they don't need or want. Equally, everyone has unfulfilled desires. It makes perfect sense to try to connect the two.

This generation has seen a revolution in the way that people are connected. The Internet allows people to meet each other's needs in a way not imagined just thirty years ago. But there's a broader perspective here too. Everyone is familiar with the idea of a collective unconscious – a kind of mutual societal awareness – yet it doesn't seem to come into play much in daily life. It ticks over in the background, but we don't actively put it into practice.

Swapping is a way of bringing this collective awareness out into the open; literally to meet one another. It means that we can do away with the usual retail chain, replacing it with an inter-relatedness of needs. And, in the process, we tap into our own primitive need to connect with our peers and our community.

Viewed in this way, it becomes clear that swapping is not just about finding practical solutions, although it is that, of course, as well. Swapping will not only get you what you need for a fraction of the retail cost, but will also bring great internal value to you, filling you with a type of satisfaction rarely experienced in the retail experience.

## Swap shopping for swapping

Swapping is a great option for anything that can't be sold. There are some really good websites turning more and more of us into keen swappers. Some do straight swaps, some ask for jobs to be done in return for things, others let you build up points for things sold so you can purchase items at a later date. Just beware of using these websites to swap your things for others you don't need; use them to get rid of your detritus and swap for anything that you really need and now realise you cannot afford to buy.

# Become a seller, not a buyer

Now that you've sorted through all your belongings, you can start to make some serious money out of them.

## Internet auction sites

If you have been an overspender on the online auction sites, you'll be very well placed to make an excellent seller if you put your mind to it. It is likely that you will already have spent hours researching without realising it; you'll know the market, have a good idea of how much things go for and what you like and dislike about how other people display their items.

Get a friend or your partner to help you photograph, price and download all your items for sale onto the site. Most sites provide an easy-to-follow guide and if you have a digital camera it's not hard to put things up for sale at all. Then monitor your sales. It can get to be even more thrilling logging on to see how much other people are bidding for your old leather jacket than it was checking whether your own buying bid was successful.

If, however, you really can't cope with setting it all up you can always take your unwanted stuff down to one of the many high-street Internet shops. They will collect your items if you can't drop them off, then they will take photographs, write descriptive listings for them and answer any questions from potential buyers. When your items are sold they will send you a cheque. They do take a fee though. So it pays to give up a Saturday when you would have been out shopping to work it out for yourself!

Here are some tips for selling on the Internet auction sites:

- Do take a good photo or three. Items that are pictured sell on average for 20 per cent more than those with only a written description.

- You can set your auction to last for up to ten days. Make sure you set it so it ends at a time when there is heavy usage on the sites, i.e. lunchtime, all day Saturday or Sunday evenings, because you want a frenzy of last-minute bids to drive up the price of your item. Avoid ending times when popular TV programmes are on, as people will be relaxing rather than bidding.

- Provide a good service. Buyers are encouraged to write a review of your product description, the time it took for you to send them their item and much more, so if you want to be a seller with a high approval rating make sure you respond to any orders promptly and efficiently.

- Check out the sites to see what items are selling and what items are most frequently searched for. Be aware of seasonal hits, so if you have a great surfboard to sell in November, keep it until next spring, and sell your Christmas stuff in early December.

## Car boot sales

This can be a really easy way to sell some of your goods. The key to successful car boot sales is to be well prepared, as you will be operating among experienced car booters as well as professional traders. So do your homework and go to a few sales before you turn up to sell.

First you need to register as a personal seller, then you will need a table to set things out on. The better your display, the more likely people are to come over and take a look. Put prices on things so that people can browse and don't have to keep checking costs with you.

If you are selling electrical goods, be aware that people might want you to demonstrate that they actually work. If you are selling children's toys, make sure you give them a good inspection to check there are no sharp edges or small parts that can be pulled off. If you have the original packaging with the instructions for any item keep it all together. If you are selling DVDs, videos, CDs or cassettes you must ensure that what you are selling is genuine. It's a good idea to take a portable DVD player with a battery so that people can check the quality of any discs before buying.

Be prepared for an early start. Most serious sellers arrive at about 7 a.m. for the big sales, so that they are ready for when the buyers arrive. Smaller boot sales tend to start a bit later on.

Also, be prepared to drop your prices towards the end of the sale. Make a big sign announcing discounts – 20, 30 or 50 per cent off everything – and put it up rather than writing out new individual price tags.

## Local free advertising

For bigger items that are hard to lug about, contact local newspapers or their websites and post a free ad. Most buyers are usually happy to arrange to transport items themselves.

If you don't like the idea of people coming to your home, put the item in the garage and take some photos to email to potential buyers. That way you know that whoever comes to view is a pretty serious buyer. You could also offer them a 10 per cent discount if they take it away there and then.

## Benjamin – addicted to selling

Sounds like good advice, doesn't it? But, as with so many things, the difficult part is actually doing it.

But being the seller and not the buyer need not be so much of a change as you might expect. It really just involves a shift of mental attitude from what you consider valuable to you in your life. You need to start seeing your money as valuable, and giving it away as a negative. Then you will start to view receiving other people's money as a big positive.

Once you get used to being your own retail tycoon, you will find that it becomes as exciting as the shopping you thought you couldn't live without. This often happens with all types of behaviour. Habits are hard to break, but once we do, the thrill of jumping out of our self-defeating box can become almost addictive.

Finding a new way to be in the world is exciting. Just be careful not to overdo it though. The key, as with so many behaviour modifications, is to find your balance. Start slowly but surely, gradually building up the changes in your life. Set yourself a target – say a certain amount to sell in a month – and try not to go over or under it. Keep going in this way until you think you are getting the right balance of novelty versus long-term sustainability.

## Renting

A new but growing concept is to rent things you want rather than buying them. And it works both ways, so you could therefore make some money renting out stuff you are not going to miss. Community websites are springing up daily as more and more people rent out items to make a profit, rather than leaving them to gather dust at the back of their garage.

# CASE STUDY

Kerry had recently separated from her boyfriend and she was up to her eyes in debt. She needed help.

It wasn't that she didn't have the capacity to make money. On the contrary; in a sense she had the potential to be relatively wealthy in that she had a home, equity and an income from a job that she liked. But she was organising her life and her affairs in such a way that she was simply spending far more money than she earned and, as a result, was having to take out huge loans which would probably have to be paid off from the equity in her house eventually.

Her home revealed a wardrobe stuffed with clothes that she'd never worn and many other items that appeared to be hardly used, if at all. So here was a person holding on to lots of things she didn't need and, in so doing, sabotaging the one thing she really did need after her recent break-up: security.

On the surface, it's tempting to say that Kerry's problem seemed to stem from adjusting to the recent separation and single life. We can all go a bit crazy when life is difficult and resort to compensating behaviours – going out, spending more money, having fun – to pick ourselves up.

But in Kerry's case, the behaviour went beyond that. There was no sense of perspective and, on analysis, another side of Kerry's life became apparent suggesting that her spending was really just a sign-post to a more complicated emotional reality.

Kerry also had issues around food. Her weight was ballooning and she was bingeing more and more on unhealthy foods. It seemed as though everything was just a little bit out of control, with a parallel between the way her body was beginning to look and the way her home looked. They both contained more than they needed and at this point her issues really began to look systemic, rather than just practical.

It was clear that this was a very extreme example of how emotional or psychological issues can influence a person's finances. The original concern was about money, but looking beyond the superficial problem, a deeper issue emerged and in order to deal with the former and getting Spendsmart, the latter had to be tackled first.

Kerry revealed a troubled family history, particularly in her early childhood. There had been a number of bereavements in the family, most significantly, perhaps, a stillborn child less than two years before her own birth. Kerry identified a long-standing feeling that something in her life just wasn't right. She'd never really been able to put her finger on it and these were not things that had been discussed at any length in her family; they were just events that had become known to her from chance comments by relatives and friends over the years.

On investigation of the possibility that there was a connection between this feeling and what was happening with her life and her money, it seemed logical, perhaps, that it would make certain times – such as the end of a relationship – particularly hard to manage. Kerry was carrying a background sense of something not being quite right, yet not knowing what that was (or what to do about it and how to feel about it), so that when she was thrust into a very difficult situation and left, essentially, on her own to manage it, resorted to coping mechanisms that were very short term (that new dress or that extra pudding at dinner), which only ever got her through the next five or ten minutes and left her with a legacy of money and weight problems.

What Kerry really required was an action plan that addressed her real core issues; she had to know what to *do*. It became clear that the part of her that really called for transformation was not her style, but her soul.

She needed to go and talk to her mother about what actually happened and how people were feeling around her as a baby and in her childhood. This revealed quite a lot of surprises, and the knowledge Kerry acquired helped her to understand her feelings a lot better. She was no longer dealing with something abstract that she could not define, and she could now understand where her feelings came from and where that innate sense of discomfort originated.

Because we are afraid of the unexplained, as soon as our conscious mind makes sense of something, it is far less threatened by it. And that's what happened to Kerry. She finally realised that 'stuff' doesn't work. She wasn't helping herself by amassing piles of clothes. What she really needed was the opposite – the space to explore who she was and to understand her real needs, which she then went about dealing with in exactly the right way.

# Look at where you could be wasting money and stop

There is no point in going to all this effort to clear up your home and raise some money if your regular outgoings are causing you to waste money. So here is a quick guide to checking your out-goings and making sure you are not letting any precious pennies go to waste. It may sound like a boring exercise, but think about it: would you rather go without something you really want because you don't have the cash to buy it, or raise the money you need from utilities savings so that you *can* afford it?

So put aside half an hour to double-check your outgoings on the following:

1. Drip spending
2. Insurance policies
3. Communications
4. Utilities
5. Car costs
6. Your home

## 1. Drip spending

Often, it's the small but regular – and unnecessary – outgoings that add up and cause trouble.

## CASE STUDY

Mary knew she had a problem with her money because at the end of every month there wasn't any! But she just couldn't get to the bottom of where it went. She wasn't extravagant. She lived a relatively quiet and unassuming life. She was just 'normal'. So where had the zero bank balance come from?

It was all the little things. It turned out that something as simple as breakfast was really sabotaging Mary's financial equilibrium. She had to be in at work quite early, so she'd get ready quickly, then grab a coffee and something to go with it on her way to work. As she was still half asleep most mornings, the cost of this never really registered. But on analysis, it was really quite surprising.

Paying out for breakfast every morning (and sometimes snacks on the way home too!) was adding up to a huge sum, and this was for things she could prepare at home for pennies. And that was just a fraction of her needless 'drip' spending. Mary was overbudget before she'd even started her working day. So vigilance is the key!

Think about your daily habits and make sure you are not guilty of any drip spending. Look carefully into all your standing orders and direct debits as well. Cancel any expensive gym memberships that don't get used, monthly payments for TV movie channels you don't watch, etc.

## 2. Insurance policies

Insurance should be simple, but these days there is a whole range of policies out there that are just not worth the money and many of yours could almost certainly be cancelled right now. They are probably quite expensive and it is doubtful that they would ever pay out if you made a claim.

## Payment protection schemes

You will have been offered payment protection schemes when you took out credit cards or a loan. The chances are that they won't pay out if you are self-employed, have a part-time job, are unable to work due to a pre-existing health problem or if you are working on a short-term contract.

## Extended warranties

Look into any extended warranties that you may have been sold for electrical appliances – they often only give you the same protection that you get for free by law anyway. Plus, most modern appliances will not break down frequently enough to balance the cost of your warranty payments.

## Insurance for your mobile phone

These policies vary and can add up to more than the cost of your phone in the case of a basic handset. Your policy may cover the cost of calls if your phone is stolen, but only if you report it within twenty-four hours and not if it was left unattended. Don't bother with these unless you are really careless or are out all the time at clubs and pubs, which is where most phones are stolen.

## Insurance for your wedding

This will pay out if the photographer forgets to show or if all the guests get food poisoning, but not if one of you changes your mind! Choose companies with reasonable cancellation policies, otherwise don't bother.

## ID theft insurance

Sales of shredders have hit the roof since we've all become worried about putting anything in our rubbish bins that has our name on it. For a monthly charge, insurance companies will check your credit for you and also that no one is taking out loans or opening new bank accounts in your name. But what they don't tell you is that you can log on to any of the credit agencies listed on p. 225 and, for a tiny fee, check all this out yourself.

### Health insurance

If you are taking out private health insurance, make sure that it is going to pay out for what you actually need. Most of the large companies won't pay out for anything to do with pregnancy and childbirth, depression, chronic diseases like diabetes and asthma or if you get MS or Alzheimer's, nor will they pay out for claims on pre-existing conditions. They only pay a percentage of the cost of treatment from osteopaths and physiotherapists. If you were in a car crash or had an accident, you would not be taken to a private hospital in any case, so quiz them hard about what your monthly insurance premium is actually going to do for you.

## 3. Communications

### Telephone and Internet

Work out if it is still worthwhile having a landline. Some people find it is cheaper to use their mobile instead of paying the line rental that is a standing charge, even if they don't use their home phone.

Don't assume that a shared Internet and telephone line means a better deal. It's complicated to work it all out, but beware that companies that give you a cheap deal for something like broadband make their money by charging you a lot for calling mobiles (and vice versa). Check every offer carefully or ask friends for recommendations and learn from their mistakes.

Get your old telephone bills out and work out where your money has been going. Do you make a lot of calls abroad? Do you call friends on mobiles? Do you make most of your calls in the evening or at the weekend? Once you highlight your main telephone spending area and what your habits are, you will know where to concentrate on saving money and how to select a deal that suits your lifestyle.

Once you have got your main package sorted you can think about cutting the costs down further still with something called an 'override provider'. These are companies that give you a phone number to dial to connect to their network, after which you make your call without any other costs. Once you have got your override number, just programme it into your phone so you don't have to dial it every time. Deals from these providers change all the time so it's best to keep an eye out to see who is offering the best rates. Also, check out those that allow calls to other countries from your landline.

## Skype

Skype is a VoIP (Voice-over-Internet Protocol) provider. Never mind what that really means – it's just a great way to talk to people if you have a computer, and means you can make free calls to other Skype account holders anywhere in the world. So it's worthwhile for you and your friends to sign up.

To do this, you need to log on and register. Then you sign up, receive a number and within a few minutes you can get going. You can choose between buying a headset or a telephone that plugs into your computer. The quality of the line does depend on your system – the faster the Internet connection the clearer the line. It also has facilities for three- or four-way conversations, customised ring tones, call waiting and voicemail.

Should you want to use it to call people who do not have Skype you would need to set up an account to buy pre-paid 'Skypeout minutes', rather like putting minutes on a pre-paid mobile. It accepts credit cards and PayPal and it does *not* allow you to put much credit on at one time – so it's a good way of keeping your costs in check. The costs of calls are extremely low and it's free to join with no monthly fees.

## Benjamin – talk is not cheap

One easy way to cut down on phone bills is to talk less. But why is that so hard for some people?

As humans, we have an innate need to relate to other people and for some this is explored more vigorously than others. We all can think of someone who can talk for England, or we may happen to be that person ourselves. And for any of us, chatting away on the phone to friends and family can be a welcome diversion from whatever is going on around us.

But the advent of the mobile phone has meant that we can sometimes miss out on opportunities for what may be difficult but interesting new conversations. Take a ride in taxi, for example – whereas passengers might have talked to the driver in the past, they now talk to friends on a mobile, while the driver does the same. We usually follow the path of least resistance in life, which in the case of the taxi ride means talking to a friend rather than striking up a conversation with someone we don't know well. And not only does this mean missing out on meeting and exploring new people, it also means spending money.

So give it a second thought when you pick up your mobile phone to chat. Is there someone already there with you who you could talk to instead? It might be harder work, but the rewards will be there, both personally and financially.

## Television

Most people who have digital TV don't watch even 10 per cent of the channels that are on offer, nor do they update or alter their package once they have signed up.

Work out what you really watch and what you would not miss. Shop around and see what deals are on offer and don't be afraid to call your existing supplier and say that you want a better deal. If they refuse, tell them you are going to cancel your subscription and, chances are, they'll miraculously find a better option for you. They really don't like losing customers, so if you stand your ground you will probably win.

Do remember that if you have taken out a TV package that includes a telephone and/or Internet service, it is likely that you will be paying way over the odds for the extra service, so explore carefully how to get out of your existing deal.

## Mobile phones

The amount of information you need to understand with regard to providers, services, tariffs and extras is completely overwhelming and not at all customer friendly. On the whole, providers will go out of their way *not* to explain anything to you, and the only way to deal with them is to play them at their own game, by calling them regularly to say that you are going to leave them. That seems to be the only language they understand, and will usually prompt them to inform you of marvellous new deals of which you had previously been un-aware. All mobile phone companies exploit the fact that most people don't manage their accounts very well. Don't pay more than you need to – take ten minutes to sit down and under-stand your mobile contract.

If you are paying through the nose for your mobile because

you don't understand your deal or can never be bothered to work out your tariff, here are some tips on sorting it out:

## Check out different providers

It is not hard to switch providers these days, so don't be put off. If you do change networks you *can* keep your number, but it may take them some time to sort it out and you may be allocated another number in the meantime. But that should not be a reason for sticking with an expensive plan you can't afford.

## Check your own deal

Check with your own network if you are on the best deal or whether you can change to a better one. If they say no and you are in a contract you can't afford, you can take your number to a new provider and carry on just paying the monthly fee you signed up for with your old provider until the contract comes to an end. If you are on a low tariff and it is the volume of calls or text messages you make that give you a high bill, this could work out nicely for you and gets you out of something that no longer suits you.

## Work out how you run up your bill

Before you decide on and sign up for a new tariff you need to look at how you use your phone. Go over old bills or call your provider and ask them to help you. Look at the following areas:

- The number of calls you make – can you make less?
- The number of calls you make to other networks – if all your friends are with different providers, can you find a good cross-package deal? If the majority of your calls are to one particular network, maybe you should move to that one?

- Text messages – don't assume they are cheap. They can really add up, so look for a deal that gives you something called a 'bundle', whereby you pay for a total amount every month. Work out how many you have been using and look for the right deal for these.

- Be aware that as soon as you go over your allowance they really charge you.Look for deals that offer a 'roll-over' so that if you have not used up your quota of minutes or texts they roll over to the next month.

## Mobile phone packages – how to pick the right one

*Contract deals*

Whatever you do, and whichever package you sign up for, ignore any cash-back or flashy upgrade deals. Concentrate on the tariffs, not the shiny, new handset or minimal cash with which they are trying to tempt you. Resist the temptation and avoid getting locked into a contract that does not work for you for up to eighteen months.

*Pay-as-you-go options*

If you have a bad credit rating this might be the only option available to you. It means paying in advance with vouchers or an electronic top-up card. The vouchers are easy to get hold of, but if you are not in a city you might need to plan ahead to ensure that you don't run out at a crucial moment. Pay-as-you-go deals are quite cost-effective if you use fewer than 150 minutes a month, but over and above that it works out as a pretty bad deal.

*SIM-only monthly deals*

Available from all the major providers, these deals are fairly new and can be a really good way to cut down your bills. They are similar to the pay-monthly contracts, but you don't have to sign up for twelve or eighteen months, and the deals are straight-forward, offering real value for money. Instead of getting a new phone, you are given a new SIM card that you can put in an existing phone. And the joy is that if you find you can't afford your deal you can cancel it with just thirty days' notice. You will need to pass a credit check, however, which might be a problem.

*Using an unwanted phone*
If you have a friend who has a phone they are not using, you can take that to a provider and just buy a SIM card to go in it. This is cheaper than signing up for a phone package.

Most younger people see their phone as a status symbol and are much more likely to upgrade regularly or even buy the latest model. That means they probably have several phones lying around the house, so they are the ones who'll be most likely to provide you with a free handset!

If you can find a free phone to use, be aware also that you can get some cash back if you sell your old mobile.

## Using a mobile phone abroad

Don't pay a fortune to you use your phone abroad. Make sure you understand what the rates are – and, as before, don't think your phone provider is going to make that easy for you. They want you to just keep on chatting wherever you are.

The simplest way to keep your bills down is to leave your mobile at home. If you can't do that, consider using text messages instead of talking – you are not charged for receiving texts when you are away, only for sending them. Text the number of your hotel to family or friends so they can call you there, and for outgoing calls use your hotel room phone rather than your mobile, but only with a pre-paid local phone card.

Turn your voicemail off so no one can leave you a message – you're charged a high rate to listen to these, so updates from a chatty friend who leaves long messages can cost you dear.

### Check out add-on packages

Before you go away, contact your provider to see whether they need to activate your phone to make it usable abroad and what their call charges abroad will be. Check all of this before you make your decision.

Ask them about their add-on packages which give you cheaper calls abroad. Be aware that these deals are only available if you connect to a provider abroad that is compatible with them. Your phone may not automatically connect to the preferred provider so you will need to know how to do this manually. Also keep an eye on it, as if you are travelling around it can suddenly change to another provider without you realising and will cost you much more.

If you do sign up with your provider for an add-on package, check whether you have to pay for it on an ongoing basis, or if you can just pay for the month you actually need it.

### Buy a pay-as-you-go phone at your destination

If you travel to a particular country frequently it may work out better in the long term to buy a phone to use when you are there (especially if it is the USA). It makes life very easy – just buy a basic handset, leave a message on your regular number saying that you are away and giving your mobile number abroad and use pre-paid top-up cards while you're there. The US phone companies are especially generous, giving you top-ups for free regularly and cards are readily available in drugstores, kiosks and garages everywhere.

*Use your own phone but buy a phone card*
If you want to stick with your own phone, buy a local phone card when you get your destination – they're available at kiosks at airports or you can pre-buy them on the Internet. Check out the rates in advance.

*Buy a stand-alone SIM card*
If you go abroad to lots of countries, the cheapest option is to use different SIM cards in your phone that you buy in whichever country you go to. Or you can buy an international or global SIM which is more expensive but will pay for itself if you are a frequent traveller.

---

## How to unlock your mobile phone

To use a different SIM card in your existing handset you will have to make sure that your phone is unlocked. Some phones come locked so that you can only use a SIM from the same network, but there is no law against unlocking it. Different providers have different charges for unlocking, or you can do it yourself for free.

To test if your phone is locked, borrow a friend's SIM card and put it in your phone. If it works, the phone is unlocked; if it says 'Restricted', you will need to unlock it, which you can do by simply following the instructions on the unlock websites.

---

## Benjamin – finding the courage to do it

Let's face it. Opening your post is a pretty grim task most of the time. Generally speaking nowadays anything you want to hear about you're unlikely to get through the letter box. So why not just push everything into a drawer and forget about it? After all, if it's really important someone will contact you another way. Won't they?

Only you can't just 'forget about it'. You'd like to think you can, but you can't. The letters are still there, and you know they are. The bills are unopened. The charges are unknown. The deadlines are not dealt with. Your idea that by ignoring them you make them less powerful is deluded, and the exact opposite is true.

Fear is often our greatest enemy. Through it we allow all sorts of things to become more of a threat to us than they really are. In the end, everything is subjective since we experience it through the filter of our mind. So if our mind is fearful, we will experience threats as more severe. You can see this, for example, in our reaction to terrorism. Many more people die of cancer than from acts of terror, and yet there is something about the pure randomness of terrorism that has us spending more time and money trying to counter it than the relatively more predictable causes of cancer. Society's reactions to these two killers shows that we are not always making logical decisions based on statistics, but emotional ones based on our tolerance of fear.

So those unopened letters hidden away in your kitchen drawer become more powerful the more you ignore them; the not knowing is far more dangerous than the information that they contain. There's nothing in them that you can't deal with, there is no situation that you can't find a way out of and there's no threat that you're not equal to handling. The difficult part is conquering your fear of finding out just how bad things have got.

The mind works in baffling ways sometimes. We have layer upon layer of defences to screen us from what's difficult to bear or to confront. But we also have magnificent resources, allowing us to achieve easily what most other species struggle to do every day of their lives: we survive relatively effortlessly in the modern Western world. We have great strength and capability. We should not fear that we can't find a way to get from one place to another in our lives. But we do.

Once again, we see how the mind is so afraid of what it does not yet know. It's like looking at the width of a chasm we have to jump across – until we are prepared to recognise and accept how wide it is, we can't make an appropriate plan for traversing it. So it is with your financial affairs.

But take heart. You can and have done many, many difficult things in your life. This is no harder, and is probably a lot easier. Just open the letters, demystify the information, find out where you've been and where you need to go; and be confident that you'll find a way to get there.

It's not hard. It's just scary . . .

## 4. Utilities

It is really easy to switch energy supplier and you can save a fortune. The comparison sites are eager to win your business and, depending on when you use them, deals can include cash-back offers or cases of wine. In your position it's advisable to go for the cash-back option here!

Try to do your switch online as you get better deals than you would by phoning them up.

The biggest discount is when you switch suppliers for the first time. Some do a special offer when you switch both gas and electricity accounts, but others don't, so don't assume that changing both will be for the best. It's a competitive market and rising fuel costs mean that your current provider may well be doing a deal where you can cap your bills in order to keep your business.

If you have a gas or electricity meter that you use a key or card for then you should get rid of it – it's like a pay-as-you-go mobile in that you never get the best rates on this service. Much better to get a regular account and pay by direct debit. Paying a new supplier on a monthly direct debit can get you a further discount of up to 10 per cent as you will be viewed as a reliable customer and unlikely to fall behind with payments. If you end up paying too much they'll just refund you at the end of the year, which is a good system for overspenders.

If you live on your own and are worried about being over-charged, make sure you check your meter every time you get a bill and call your supplier with the correct reading, so they can amend their files and not continue to bill you according to their estimates (which may well be based on the average family's consumption).

*How to reduce your energy bills*
There are lots of things you can do to make sure you keep your bills down and it can make you feel good being green, too:

- Turn your thermostat down.
- Only boil as much water in the kettle as you actually need.
- Install cavity wall insulation. Any house built after the 1920s can have this done and it should save you a lot.
- Top up loft insulation to around 25 cm.
- Place reflective sheets behind radiators to make sure heat gets out into your rooms and does not just escape through the walls.
- Replace ordinary light bulbs with energy-saving ones.

- Make sure you only buy energy-saving appliances.
- Get some flexible foam strip draught excluders which you can stick to door or window frames.
- Fit an interior flap on your letter box and add a bristled threshold excluder to your door frame base to warm up a chilly hall.
- Fill gaps in the skirting with Unibond.
- Pile on cosy sweaters and slipper socks.
- Draw the curtains as soon as it is dusk, and get a cheap, heavy lining for them if necessary to keep draughts out.
- Turn your TV and computer off, rather than leaving them on standby.
- Defrost your fridge/freezer regularly. It is the hardest-working appliance in your home, so don't leave the door open for long periods, never put hot food straight into it and make sure the door seals are secure.
- Put beds against the inside walls to stay snug.
- Only ever run the washing machine on full and on the lowest temperature setting. Also get some 'ecoballs' – they produce ionised oxygen that lets water penetrate deep into the fibres of clothes to lift dirt so you can use less washing powder. They can be used a thousand times and come with refills.
- Don't tumble dry – get a clothes line and some pegs and hang washing outside.
- Check out devices that connect to your fuse box and display your energy usage – just watching the total going up acts as a big incentive for many to cut right back.

## Water bills

Don't think for a second that what you pay for your water bill reflects accurately what you use. Water company charges are based on your home's 'rateable value', i.e. the money your house could be rented out at. It is a stupid system and if you live alone, or with a partner, it can really pay to ask your supplier to install a meter so that you can reduce your bills. The water company has to install a meter if you request it.

# 5. Car costs

### Insurance

Take advantage of the fact that this is a highly competitive area, so it should be easy to save some money here. Check the comparison sites and take your time, making sure you fill in all the forms to the letter. Be very specific about your job title and if the descriptions don't fit what you do, find a site for one where it does – don't get pushed into a similar occupation bracket where costs can be significantly higher.

Be aware that buying a security device for your car can lower your premium, as can not having drivers under the age of twenty-five on your policy. Be precise about where you park – if it's in a garage or in a private driveway this can make costs lower than if it's on a public road overnight.

Look at your mileage too; many insurers now do good policies if you drive fewer than 6000 miles a year. Also, if you are retired, are a woman, have no claims or don't use your car for work you can get better deals, so be sure to give them every bit of information that might lower your premium.

### Petrol

Never go for the overpriced super-plus options at the garage – it's just not worth your while. Also, prices change frequently, so don't assume that the local garage you went to last time is still the cheapest. Keep checking. (There are websites that can tell you where to get the cheapest petrol in your area at any given time.)

# 6. Your home

## Insurance

Don't think that you have to wait until your policy is up for renewal to change insurance companies. If you have not made a claim on it you should be able to cancel whenever you want and get a full refund if you find something much better.

If you own your own home you will probably have two insurance policies to cover your home – buildings and contents. You can buy these separately or together, but it is always best to start with separate quotes as you may be considered high risk for one and not the other. If there is not much difference you might decide to use the same company for both, just to cut down on admin.

If you are renting, it's your landlord's responsibility to cover the building and their own goods, i.e. anything owned by them that is listed on the itinerary such as carpets, vacuum cleaners, white goods and so on, but it is up to you to take out your own contents insurance. You can ask the landlord to provide adequate locks on the doors and windows to make sure you qualify for a better rate and they should, by law, install a smoke alarm and provide gas and electricity safety certificates.

Try to do whatever you can to ensure that you fall into a low risk category. Think about:

- joining a Neighbourhood Watch scheme
- making sure all windows have approved window locks fitted
- installing approved locks on your front and back doors, one being a mortise lock
- installing a burglar alarm.

You can also offer to pay the first £50 or £100 of a claim, and should tell the insurance company if you have a dog, are a non-smoker, or work from home – these are all factors that can reduce your premium. And, as with car insurance, offering to pay by direct debit can work in your favour.

## Reduce your cleaning costs

Could you cut down on the amount of cleaning products you buy? Or, if you employ a cleaner, could you manage without? It's not that hard to keep a modern house clean and tidy once you have de-cluttered your space.

All you need is a basic vacuum cleaner, a good steam iron and ironing board, some old cloths and dusters, lemons, bicarbonate of soda, vinegar, olive oil, old newspapers and a few cheap cleaning products, and most of your problems will be solved! We are bombarded with adverts for cleaning products and gadgets, very few of which we actually need. Just ask your parents or grandparents for some good old-fashioned cleaning tips and do the job yourself. Here are some general tips to save buying expensive, often unnecessary products.

*Windows*

Wash the frames and sills with hot water and a few drops of washing-up liquid. Then get some old newspapers and dip them in a bucket of water diluted with a slug of vinegar and get wiping. Borrow a ladder from a neighbour if you don't have one yourself, and see your windows come up crystal clear and sparkling.

*Wood and furniture*

Add a few drops of lemon juice to some olive oil and use to polish wood or leather furniture. For fabric upholstery and curtains use the suction pipe attachment of your vacuum cleaner.

*Dusting*
Buy a microfibre cloth for everything including your computer and TV so that you're not just redistributing the dust before it resettles.

*Sinks*
Sprinkling some bicarbonate of soda down the sink a couple of times a month and leaving it for an hour before flushing out should keep your sink problem-free. If your drains outside are blocked, caustic soda from a hardware shop should get rid of most things, but wear gloves when you are handling it and keep the kids well away – it's really strong stuff.

*Kitchen surfaces*
Vinegar mixed with lemon juice should keep draining boards and taps sparkling. If you have any stainless steel appliances you can use baby oil to make them look as good as new.

*Ovens*
This is a job for when you're at home all day. Take out all the shelves and runners and soak them in a sink of hot water with some biological detergent that you use for your washing. Next, spread a thick layer of baking soda on the bottom of a cool oven, spray it with water until it is damp and shut the door. Repeat every few hours until the baking soda dries out. When you scrape it off, all the food residue will go with it. This stops any food that you are cooking having that horrid taste of oven cleaner, too, and leaves the whole oven sparkly.

*Toilets*
Keep them sparkling by putting some denture cleaning tablets in the bowl and leaving for a few hours before flushing away. Alternatively, use some strong bleach once week and leave overnight before flushing.

*Garden*
A little bleach in warm water and a stiff brush are great for cleaning patio stones.

## Spendsmart preparation – summary

Well done! You have now completed two of the five Spendsmart steps, and should hopefully be feeling more in control. Not only have you got a bit more used to the fact that you are in debt, you have also identified any resources and goods that you can sell to raise money towards repaying your debts. Plus, you should now be living in a home that is clutter-free, giving you more physical and emotional space.

The ideas and suggestions for cutting down on your outgoings should soon start to make a real difference and, as you move confidently on to Step Three, it's worth taking a moment to consider how far you have already come.

STEP **3** THREE

# Spendsmart Detox

## Up for the challenge

The Spendsmart detox is not designed to make you suffer! It is a proven and effective way of making you realise what you have been spending your money on, and it will provide you with vital clues. You'll see exactly when and how you overspend, you'll identify your spending triggers better, you'll get to know your shopping psyche and be equipped to stay on track throughout the remainder of the Spendsmart process.

This is the only Spendsmart step that we put a time limit on, and you need to commit to doing it for seven days. Set aside a realistic time for your detox. Christmas, a big birthday event, weddings and holidays are all times to avoid, so plan ahead and reserve seven days in which you can do this with confidence and calm.

Make sure you tell friends and family exactly what you are doing; it's going to be a long, hard seven days and the most successful detox weeks are always those where the support of others is on hand whenever and wherever it's needed most.

# Benjamin – how badly do you want this?

Before turning the page, ask yourself how committed you are to actually doing what this chapter insists on, ask yourself how seriously you've taken Spendsmart so far. Have you read sections of this book thinking, I'll come back to that later? Is this one of them? Or are you actually engaging with the advice and doing your homework? Because that's what is needed if you are to effect real change in your life. So if you are struggling with that, you might want to think about where your emotional resistance to this process is coming from.

We've seen that understanding people in general can help with understanding their specific problem behaviours. And we've also seen that money can be an emotional currency. In the same way that it plays a big part in our fantasy and our own sense of what our destiny is, it's also something that causes very strong emotional reactions. We are hardly ever emotionally neutral about money.

So if your plan is to get Spendsmart, first of all you have to understand how you feel about it, and why you haven't automatically done it already; in other words, how you feel about money and what you've been doing with it, or just how you feel, full stop. If you don't do that basic groundwork you may not be able to survive the difficulties that arise when money causes strong emotional reactions. And these difficulties are what this detox will reveal.

Money is also everywhere in relationships, and has an enormous influence on them. We've already mentioned relationships with fathers (see p. 20), but it also affects relationships with colleagues, with siblings and with children. In some ways it often serves as a measuring device; and if the measurements that are made don't correspond to how you feel and how others feel about you, this again can trigger tremendous emotional responses. To understand your spending past, you also need to understand your past relationships.

Any prior emotional baggage can make it tempting to use money in a dysfunctional way in order to avoid experiencing the feelings that lie behind the need for this behaviour. So, any broader issues that you haven't dealt with in your life may be attached to finances, to money, to wealth, and ultimately, to your capacity to become Spendsmart.

The way that our money affects us can be a huge catalyst in unearthing buried feelings, and that's something that we'll often do anything to avoid. If you're really determined to get Spendsmart you will need to deal with the financial and emotional nightmare of this detox and look really carefully at all of the feelings that come up for you during this week. This will give you a fresh perspective on both your past and future.

Each and every single one of us can find a way to be Spendsmart within our own context. It's not just about measuring the amount of money you have. If you're a person who can organise your affairs in such a way that you spend less than you earn, then by definition you are living with abundance. You will have more than you need, and that *is* the concept of abundance. But to get to this financial Shangri-la, you first need to understand how and why you've been spending in the past.

And the key to it all is turning your mental blocks into stepping stones towards the targets you set for yourself. And your detox is, perhaps, the most important step of all.

# Spendsmart detox – the rules

Work out how much you normally spend in a week on *non-essential* items (beer, magazines, extras at the garage, your weekly shopping, petrol, gadgets, DVD rentals, etc.). It's probably best to get a friend or colleague to help you come up with an honest answer here, as most overspenders are expert at wildly underestimating their weekly spend. Take the last week as an example and make a written list of everything. For some people petrol will be an essential item, but if you can walk, cycle or take the bus, for example, it really is a non-essential. Also, we all need to eat, but think about all the little luxuries you pop into your weekly supermarket shop – they really add up.

# My Spendsmart detox list of spending

(Remember that this is a list of non-essential weekly spending, so it does not include your mortgage/rent or bills.)

Supermarket shopping
Travel
Petrol
Eating out
Drinking out
Lunches at work
Coffees/snacks
Magazines
Beauty and gym
Football tickets
Exercise classes, etc.
Anything else

**In an average week I spend a total of £     on non-essential items.**

Now that you have a figure for your current weekly expenditure, you need to decide on a sum – based on whether you are single or have a family, and taking into account what you have now seen to be non-essential spends – and prepare to live on it for the next seven days. As a general rule it should be a fifth of what you normally spend. It needs to be a challenge, but don't try to be heroic as you do also have to be practical.

Take out your designated amount for the week in cash and put away all your cards and remaining money. Life is really quite simple now – for the next seven days, you can only spend the money that you have in your pocket! So get real with your spending and work out how your cash is going to last. This means making some hard choices. Think about:

- Travel – you might have to walk to the station or take the children to school on the bus instead of filling up the car.
- Eating – you can use up what is in the freezer or cook inexpensive meals instead of ordering takeaways.
- Socialising – decide whether you really want to go to the pub if you can't afford to buy a round.
- Shopping – are there any recent purchases you can take back to the shops for a refund?

Whatever choices you make over the next seven days, it is important to remember that *you* are in charge of your money for the week, albeit a nominal amount.

## Break your routine

Routines can sometimes cause massive overspends, so the more you do things differently this week the better. And the more you explore new options, the more interesting your week will be.

Remember, this exercise is only for seven days, and although it is hard you *can* do it.

## Keep a diary

Keep a diary of how you feel. Are you upset that you can't go out on a Friday or does it make you furious? Do you feel resentful when you have to deny yourself? Are you already planning a binge spend when the cold turkey is over? Whatever your feelings – write them down. They will be the clues on which we will base your future spending.

The trick to keeping a diary of your emotions is to allow them to lead you into whatever territory your mind wants to wander into. This will reveal what the reasons for your spending habits might really be.

So find yourself a notebook or a journal and dedicate it to your emotional diary. It can be a fresh notebook or something that you already use – the main criterion is that it is sufficiently portable that you can take it with you wherever you go and have it with you at *all* times.

You are going to use this journal instead of your credit cards when the spending mood takes you. As soon as you feel that you are about to be overwhelmed by a spending urge, you take out your journal and try to write down exactly how you are feeling. Slow down the experience so that you can access the urges and the emotions themselves. What kicked off the urge? Can you identify a specific trigger? Was it a conversation with someone, or a thought you had? Dig as deep as you can, and find the feelings that you need to convey. And we want specific emotions here – are you angry? Sad? Glad? – not just a general mood, expressed by something like 'I feel that I want to shop'.

So a typical entry might begin as follows:

> I'm on the bus and I just saw a dress in a shop window. I really want to jump off the bus and go and buy it, even though I know it'll make me late for work and I can't afford it. I wonder why I feel like this?
>
> I can't buy it because I'm on my detox week and it's making me feel really upset and down. I feel sad and angry. I feel like I deserve that dress and it's not fair that I'm not able to get it. No one ever listened to me and I was always the last one to get what they needed.

This sample diary entry shows how a specific thought about needing to do something in the present can quite easily turn into a general thought about something from the past, as long as you let your mind wander and the feelings flow.

Next, you need to try to connect to the past. The easiest way to do this is to ask yourself when was the first time you remember feeling this way? So that would look like this:

> The first time I remember feeling this way was when I was about seven or eight and my whole family were at the beach for the summer holidays. I remember Dad playing with my brothers, but no one bothered with me. Mum wasn't well and when they had finished playing football Dad took the boys for an ice cream but no one thought to get me one. When they asked me if I wanted one as an afterthought I said no, but really I was desperate for one. I just wasn't going to give them the satisfaction of knowing it.

You then conclude your journal entry by acknowledging how you are feeling right now as you write it:

> Remembering all this I feel really sad, but also a bit relieved because it seems important somehow. Funnily enough I don't feel like shopping any more and I'm glad I'm still on the bus.

While you are doing this exercise, keep a note of what you *do* actually buy. Note down the things you don't buy and how much you miss having them. You will be surprised at how easy some things are to give up, while it can be impossible to say no to others.

## Topping up your detox budget

This week you can create extra money for yourself. Return something that you don't need to the shop and get a refund; call in the favour from a friend who owes you money; if your friends want you to go to a social event and are prepared to pay for you, it's your call to make, depending on how comfortable you feel about it.

## Tips for getting through the Spendsmart detox experience

### Resisting temptation

Resisting temptation can be hard. If you find that you are desperate to spend on something, try writing down the item you are lusting after and the price, and beside it a mark out of ten, representing how badly you want it. Do this whenever you want from Monday to Friday, listing as many items as you need to. Then on Saturday, study the list. You will be hard-pressed to remember more than a third of the things you thought you could not live without. This will really help you to prioritise your spending habits and highlight areas of temptation for the future. Shopping knowledge really is power.

## The 'I deserve it' syndrome

Be honest and work out how many times you overspend because you think you deserve a treat? You are more likely to think this way if you are a woman and the tougher things get, the easier it is to feel that you deserve a new pair of shoes, a leather passport holder or a hydrating facial. This is when you really need to understand how emotional shopping takes over from any question of need, and the more you indulge in magic-fix purchases, the longer you will be in debt.

The detox week hits 'I deserve it' shoppers hardest, as it reveals quite a few home truths. Rising living costs mean that there is ever less money for you to indulge in cheer-up shopping. Posh Spice can afford five hundred pairs of shoes, but you can't. Sarah Jessica Parker can change designer handbags three times a day without missing a heartbeat, but you are not in her league. It doesn't matter what your best friend has, what your neighbours are installing or what your sister's kids are wearing – you have to understand that you *cannot* continue to spend like a celebrity if your salary, your mortgage and your other financial commitments won't stretch to it.

## Explore instant access bank accounts and text-message banking

If you really need extra help, there is a basic bank account that allows you to have wages or benefits paid in to it and to take cash only out. You are not allowed chequebooks, cheque guarantee cards or an overdraft. Some allow you to have direct debits and standing orders too, which can be useful, so look at different options before making a decision.

This is quite a drastic step, but if you are finding your seven days really difficult, you may decide that drastic action is what's required in order to curb your spending in the long term.

You should also look at banks that offer accounts where you get a text message every week with your updated account balance. Some will also send you text alerts when you are nearing your limit or about to hit zero in your account.

## Give yourself small treats

If you are really missing certain things, allow yourself a small treat. Take sandwiches to work for the week and use some of the money saved for a coffee and your favourite snack on Friday. Instead of buying five magazines over the week, choose the one you like best and sit down and really enjoy it, rather than just flicking through it in just a few minutes.

## Curb your impulse spending

This is the spending you do when you see something you had not planned to buy. We looked at this and the stages leading up to it in Step One (see p. 12). You might find it harder than ever to resist impulse spending while you're doing your detox – it's that feeling of wanting something that is not on your list; you don't need it, you don't care how much it costs, *you just want it*. The trouble is that this feeling can hit overspenders quite often, so be prepared for it to happen and be aware that it will pass.

Bank statements and credit card bills are useful tools in helping you to determine what your triggers for impulse spending are. Take a look at yours and see if the same type of item appears over and over again – CDs, gadgets, online book or music store buys or clothes? One or two areas of weakness should emerge and indicate where you will need to be extra vigilant this week. If you find it hard to identify these items, think about how sometimes you feel regretful or guilty about purchasing certain things. They are usually the things that stay in the bag for three weeks while you deal with your conscience. Chances are that at this detox stage you'll be wishing you could have all the money back rather than the goods in question.

To help yourself break the compulsive spending pattern, think about the stuff that you have just cleared out of your house, and how much of that was redundant seconds after the purchase thrill. Realising that most of the stuff you splash out on has absolutely no point (beyond providing the transitory rush you experience when you buy it) is a big part of the detox week.

## The Spendsmart 'card case'

As you get used to using cash only this week, be aware that it's a habit we want you to keep up. Knowing how much money you can live on when you have to should make you more confident about being able to stick to the long-term budget that we are going to create in Step Four.

So that you don't go straight back to using your cards and not thinking about the amount you are spending on them after this week, follow the instructions below to make the Spendsmart card cases and put your cards inside them. You may well think we are crazy to suggest this, but we are deadly serious. You are in a lot of trouble with money and need all the help you can get to stop yourself spending. What these card cases do is to break your automatic See-Want-Spend pattern. When you take out a card and see that it is wrapped in a paper case, you have to think about it in a different way. And that brief moment, when you first see the card case and decide whether or not to take the card out, can be long enough to allow you to make an informed decision, rather than rush into a purchase that you can no longer afford.

(Front)

Do I really need this?

Have I got one already?

Do I have to buy other items to go with it?

Am I prepared to give something up
in order to afford this?

Can I go out of the shop for five minutes
to think it through?

(Back)

I do not want to waste my money
any more.

I want to get my money under control.

I want less stress.

I don't wish to clutter up my life with
purchases that I don't need or want.

I deserve to get what I **need** – not
what I want.

*Instructions:* Photocopy the above and cut along the solid lines. Fold along the horizontal dotted line and then fold in the side flaps and tape the edges. Run off as many copies as you need, depending on the number of cards you have (hopefully not many by this stage). Put a card inside each one (including your Switch card, if you have one).

# Recognise the link between your compulsions and your spending

## CASE STUDY

George was addicted to mini-breaks. He was a suave young man, whose urge to travel might have been understandable. But George was throwing away his inheritance on these luxuries. He always travelled well, always stayed in four- or five-star hotels, but he had nothing to show for it all besides a pile of postcards.

He was, meanwhile, training to be an accountant, and there was a very real sense that if he didn't manage to get a better grip on his own finances, he might not even have the money to carry on his training. He was also jeapordising his right to practise with the possibility that he could become bankrupt.

The interesting thing was that George was actually quite competent around money and had no problem managing it in theory. After all, he was training to be an accountant. So money did not, in itself, seem to be the driver of George's behaviour. In a way, his was a proxy financial problem because the real issue lay in George's addiction to travel. Which raised the question of what he was trying to get away from, rather than what he thought he was going towards when he went on these trips.

It turned out that George had been treated very badly in his family for being gay. His relatives had suspected that he was gay from a young age and had hurled abuse at him. Unfortunately, he had received the same treatment at school from a teacher too. He grew up feeling like the whole town was against him and that there was nowhere he felt safe. It was a very difficult way for a young man to grow up.

But when he went on his travels he was treated differently. The staff in the expensive hotels accepted him and made him feel important, almost loved, in the way he had always longed to feel as a child. So in a sense, the five-star-hotel experience became a substitute for the childhood that George should have had, regardless of whether or not he was gay.

George was paying to manufacture an emotion that he craved, or rather to remove one that he hated. On the one hand, yes, he was doing something positive, but on the other hand, he *had* to do it because it anaesthetised his pain. But, like any drug, it wore off. The moment he left the hotel, or even the moment when he had to pay the bill, he felt different; and he wasn't going to be able to afford this for ever. George was surrendering his opportunity for a wealthy and rewarding career to an addiction that met his needs, rather than by dealing with his problems on a deeper level.

George realised that if he was going to address the issues that plagued him without running away all the time, he had to go back to his home town and to his family and confront the bullies from his past. He set up a drama workshop for the local school at which he had been the victim of homophobic teachers and he got to tell his story to a new generation of more sympathetic kids and teachers. This was a great relief for him, and he suddenly began to feel that he could stop running. It had been hard for him to curb his mini-breaks, but it meant that he had found the space and courage to address the core issue and, in so doing, he realised something very powerful about the homophobia that he had seen as a child: that it was *their* problem, not his. Although it had damaged and hurt him, it didn't start with him and neither, therefore, did it have to end with him.

George continued to have a taste for travel and adventure, but was now able to make it less frequent and more in line with his budget. His problem had not been about managing his money – which he was more than capable of doing – but about managing himself.

Travel, eating out, drink, drugs, even love, can be compulsive or addictive behaviours. All of them can have a financial cost, often one that is too great for you. And you will never get rich if you're just using money to fuel a deeper need; if you're having to pay more than you can afford to manufacture feelings that you need for other reasons.

You need to get into the issues behind the habits. There are a number of standard ways to deal with compulsive and/or addictive behaviours. Detox is where you start. A lot of people find that once, having done the detox, they realise the grip their behaviours had on them and what it cost them, they then have the will power to stop. They feel that they can simply give up and try to find alternative ways of addressing the underlying problem that are less damaging, less expensive and less unhealthy.

If you really want to prioritise money and wealth, and through your detox and diary you can identify a different problem in your life that's contributing negatively to that, then it should give you the determination and the courage to begin to address the original problem.

*Note*: in cases of more serious addictions professional help is available. Psychotherapy has been seen to help, as can residential rehabilitation. And there is a variety of very helpful free twelve-step programmes along the lines of Alcoholics Anonymous for debt, overeating and all sorts of other addictions. These have been seen to be very effective at helping people who have no other resources and no other way of coping with very destructive behaviours.

## Making new personal spending rules

We all make our own rules as adults. What time we get up, which job we take, whether or not we want to have children, what we eat for breakfast, where to go on holiday, and so on. We make rules and choices for ourselves all the time, so why is it that overspenders seem incapable of making any successful shopping rules?

Here's what getting your personal spending rules right means:

- You feel in control.
- You are not getting into debt.
- You don't feel deprived by not having the things you can't afford.
- You feel confident that you have made the right choices for yourself and your bank account.

## Understanding your spending choices

It sounds straightforward enough as a concept, but understanding your spending choices is not so easy to do in your own life.

Your Spendsmart detox week will already be showing you how, when forced into changing your habits, you *can* actually do it. It should also become apparent that it is all too easy to do the same things all the time and that this can have a really negative influence on your life. Ask yourself the following questions:

- Do I watch the same TV programmes all the time?
- Do I read the same newspaper every day?
- Do I buy the same products week in, week out at the supermarket?
- Do I always buy the same round at the pub?
- Do I park in the same place at work every day?
- Do I buy the same make of jeans every time?

Can you see how readily we become creatures of habit without realising it? And how spending goes hand in hand with this?

Your detox should be helping you to see your spending possibilities as more flexible, and you have to try to remain open-minded about your habits and even look forward to creating some new, healthy ones as you complete the remainder of the Spendsmart plan. You don't have to continue with the same habits, just because you always have.

Much of this step is really about your identity and perception of yourself. People often say things to themselves like, 'I always go shopping on the weekend. That's just who I am.' So your behaviour is not just about what you do, it's also associated with your idea of who you are.

## CASE STUDY

Andy grew up in a family who went shopping on a Saturday. This was their time together – a sort of family day out. She remembers it fondly, especially how she always had a good laugh with her mother and sisters.

Now, as an adult, she feels that life is much harder. She's feels cut off from that sense of community and family, and finds that sticking to the old routine of shopping at the weekend comforts her somehow. But where there used to be laughter and banter with her family, now she is alone and uses the time to buy things that she can't afford.

Once Andy understood that she was lonely, she found this habit much easier to give up. She replaced her shopping time with social and sporting activities, like joining a netball club, and found that something that had seemed so important to her was not, actually, such a useful habit after all.

## Your personal choices – vital for success

You are learning that you cannot buy everything you want, which means making choices about what you will and will not spend on, and it is essential that you understand these choices are the key to your Spendsmart success.

Keep a record of anything you have really missed during your Spendsmart detox week, as well as those things that you expected to miss but didn't. This information will be important when it comes to putting your budget together. You will be living on less money than you have been, and knowing what you can pull back on without feeling deprived and what you are going to have to be careful about in the future is crucial.

## Benjamin – you are what you choose

Everything that we have, everything that we've ever spent money on, is something that we have chosen. Choice is a very important concept.

It can be very empowering to begin to recognise the positive choices in your life, rather than feeling that you are merely reacting to choices that have been imposed on you by the buffeting forces of the world. For example, your detox was a choice. It may feel like something excruciating that you are only doing because you were told to, but actually it was your choice. And you made that choice because you wanted to get better – to get Spendsmart.

Equally, you can see all of your spending decisions – whether to spend or not to spend – as a positive choice. Only you can decide what you are going to prioritise and what you are going to do without, and each decision you make is being made by *you*, to realise your choice to get on top of your money.

So when you decide that you will not buy a glossy magazine, don't feel deprived and depressed about not having more money. Instead, congratulate yourself on having exercised the power to choose your own destiny. You are doing this because you want to – it is your decision, and therefore your choice.

Making good choices is going to be the cornerstone of your Spendsmart life. People often make poor decisions when they are stressed, tired, worried or influenced by other people who are making bad choices themselves. If you find that perhaps you're not achieving your spending goals, look back over the choices you have made.

If making good decisions is difficult because of background problems in your life, try to slow down your decision-making process. Make a choice, but don't act on it for a day. Then revisit it and see if it still works for you.

Your new life will be based on all of the different choices you are going to make, so you need to get used to the fact that everything is a choice, and ensure that your choices fit your overall objective of getting Spendsmart.

# Is there life after detox?

## Spendsmart substitutes for shopping

From now on, you're going to need something that will give you that same feel-good hit, that same high and that same sense of accomplishment that you got when you were shopping. The fix you have been getting from overspending has become addictive, hence you have been unable to resist the urge to buy more and more things in order to feed your addiction. We need to replace that feel-good hit without it involving your wallet. It may take a bit of trial and error, but we will get there in the end.

It doesn't have to be a big thing. It could be going to an afternoon movie with a friend and having coffee and a laugh afterwards. Or taking your kids kite-flying, chatting with your mum over a cup of tea or sorting out your garden. Only you know what is most likely to work for you.

Many people find that what gives them a good feeling is being part of something. Have you ever noticed how the most interesting people to be with are those who are always interested in what is happening around them? If you're finding yourself thinking that you don't have the confidence to join a class or a group of some kind, or that you 'just can't', stop and think about what you have achieved in the last week – the Spendsmart detox was probably way outside your comfort zone, yet you've done it; and this is no different.

If you are having difficulty finding something to do instead of shopping, try thinking about what made you happy as a child and see if that's something you could do now – horse riding, for example, or taking up an old hobby again.

Or think about doing something for others – a guaranteed way to make you feel good too. There are various organisations that put potential volunteers in touch with a wide range of charities, and now that you are not out shopping all day you could put that time to good use, reading to a child for an hour a week, mentoring a student, clearing a local wildlife park – the possibilities are endless. That warm sensation you get when you have helped someone ('elevation', as it is known) is a great feeling, and it tends to hang around for a lot longer than the buzz you'd get from buying another pair of shoes!

Think about why you're doing all this. Repaying your debts and getting back in control really does matter; having a handbag that is going to date within months and costs six weeks' wages does not.

## Identify your negative spending patterns

Once you have finished your Spendsmart detox week, you should be starting to feel more in control and ready to move on to the next stage. But before you do that, we need to take some time to identify where future temptation is likely to strike.

To get an idea of where your weaknesses lie, take a look at the notes you made during your detox week of all the things you really missed, and others you missed less than you expected to. In addition, here are some scenarios that highlight negative spending habits to watch out for.

### Did you miss spending in front of your friends?

It's amazing how some people can get vicarious pleasure out of seeing another person overspend. And the fact that *you* got a real thrill from overspending in front of your friends probably suited them just fine – it meant they didn't have to! So while you may well have felt odd this last week not being the one impressing the crowd, now that you've had a break from social spending to impress, keep it up.

Look at your group of friends and at how everyone is given a label – the bad one, the one who is always late, the flirt, the crazy one, the big spender, the killjoy, and so on. Note also how people always seem to live up to the labels they are given. Be careful not to let the expectations of others make you overspend in order to please them. It's time to choose another label that you are comfortable with. Try the sensible one, the one who is sorting out their money, and see how that feels.

## Did you miss spending on socialising?

A lot of people on their Spendsmart detox week find it easier to cut out socialising altogether, rather than cut back. If your friends chose to subsidise you through your detox, how did that make you feel? Did you feel comfortable knowing that they were helping? Did it make you feel cross that they could afford things that you can't? Whatever your feelings, being honest with your friends about your situation from now on will make things a lot easier.

Habits mean that we tend to go to the same places with the same friends and order the same food and drinks. But if you want to carry on socialising you are going to have to break some of those habits. Maybe you could drink less, take public transport home or just go out less often? Whatever compromise or change you choose to make, remember that it is your choice and has to work for you in the long term; and that making no change at all is no longer an option.

## Did you miss spending in your favourite shops?

It's strange how many people go to the shops as a way of relaxing. But in your case, you know deep down that it is really not going to help you. It was easy enough in the past to kid yourself that a potter around the shops was just a pleasant way to spend your lunch hour, or to pass time at the weekend if you were bored or even just lonely. But in reality, to get your fix you always had to buy something even if you'd sworn to yourself that you wouldn't.

Stay away from shops altogether if you feel angry, sad, fat or lonely. Get in the habit of going to visit a friend or calling them instead.

## Did you miss spending on your children?

If you have been overspending on your children, it can be hard to stop, and you will probably come up with all sorts of reasons to justify why you should continue: it's not like you're spending money on yourself; they shouldn't suffer because of your problems; they need things, and so on.

It's all too easy to give yourself yet another reason why you need to spend money on them, but chances are they really don't *need* anything else. Don't be afraid to explain to your children that you are on a cutback and are having to be much more careful with money. Tell them that from now on you are going to give them their own pocket money, and tell them this is a positive change. If they are not going to make overspending mistakes as adults, children need to learn the value of money. So give them each an old-fashioned piggy bank, a set amount of pocket money, maybe with an option to earn more by doing odd jobs around the house and garden (see p. 147), and see how quickly they learn to appreciate just what's involved in saving up for a new Nintendo DS game. It's neither cruel nor unreasonable to say no to them: it's just sensible parenting.

## Did you miss spending on clothes?

Clothes can be an easy fix for an overspender, but it is amazing how much junk we can accumulate before we feel enough is enough. Ask yourself how happy you are with your body, as low body esteem is a guaranteed reason for endless spending. You just never seem to find that perfect item to make you look thinner/taller/ smaller/curvier/cooler/richer, and that search has ended in bankruptcy for many people.

When you go post-detox clothes shopping you should keep a few sensible tips in mind. Go shopping on your own so that you can concentrate on finding things that really do fit you and realise that if you are taller, shorter, fatter or thinner than the norm, it will take you much longer to find things. Don't go shopping on Saturdays when the stores are packed and the whole experience becomes stressful. Never shop with friends who are thinner or richer than you, and never buy clothes without trying them on. Don't make the mistake of overspending on accessories, bags or shoes because you can't find anything to fit. It is not the answer.

## Benjamin – missing *you*

By now you may be overwhelmed by a sense of loss as you find yourself missing so many of the familiar components of your life. That's quite normal. One of the dark secrets of getting straight with your money lies in the fact that you are going to have to grieve for the person you were before, and the things that he or she used to do. Change is often desirable, but it's also always difficult.

In dealing with the problem of saying goodbye to the old you before you can really move on, it may help to understand the five stages of grief. They don't always come in this order, and you won't necessarily experience all of them, but it is generally accepted that letting go involves at least two of these steps:

## Denial

You might have moments when you think that all of this isn't really happening, or doesn't need to happen. You're fine with your money; everyone has a few problems; you don't need to change; it's not worth it. That's denial.

## Anger

It's not fair – why me? You may be overtaken by a sense of out-rage and fury about the changes that are seemingly being forced upon you. Feeling that you are boxed in and unable to avoid the changes that you dread can provoke some really strong feelings of rage.

## Bargaining

Often, this is a response to the denial and anger. Once the shock and fury wear off there is a desire to try to wriggle out of your very difficult situation. You say things like, 'If I just get half of my debt paid off, I can carry on as before and don't need to change too much for too long.' But this is missing the point. It's not your money that needs to change, but you. And that means letting go in order to move on.

## Depression

When avoiding the problem has clearly failed, the bleakness of what's happening can be overwhelming. You might wonder what the point is, or feel that you just can't go on. This is actually a healthy stage of grief, and a normal reaction to loss. It shows that you have moved on from the first three stages.

## Acceptance

Once you've had enough of feeling sorry for yourself, you'll have to get on with the rest of your life. At this point, most people just shrug, wonder what all the fuss was about and start again. This marks the successful transition from one identity into another.

Give yourself time to arrive at acceptance, and also be aware that you can go back and forth through these stages, sometimes straddling two at once. Just go with the process. In time you'll get used to the new you and won't regret all the self-destructive parts of your identity that you've left behind.

# Don't let the shops manipulate you

You are almost ready for Spendsmart Step Four now, but before we sort out your new budget and let you loose in the shops again, you need to understand just how easily you can be manipulated out there. Shops today deploy many tricks to make you spend money, and knowing their game can make it a lot easier to resist spending. You're feeling more in control of your money and spending now, so don't allow the shops to undo all your hard work.

## How do shops make you spend more money?

An overspender is the perfect customer as they are more likely to:

- linger in the shop for longer
- buy more than they'd intended
- shop without a list
- be more susceptible to marketing tricks.

If you are tempted to spend, just stop and ask yourself whether you really want to let a shop get the better of you. You wouldn't let a friend do it, so why allow a high-street store? Can you really afford to continue being a victim of manipulation?

So before entering any shop, work out how long (if at all) you need to be in there for, and what you need to buy. The longer you are in a shop, the more you are likely to spend, and shops will encourage you to linger – relaxing background music, pleasant lighting and widely spread merchandise are all geared towards keeping you in the shop for longer than you'd intended and making you walk around more of it. Some stores even black out or remove windows, so that you lose sight of the outside world.

Department stores in particular will lay out paths for you to follow, leading you where *they* want you to go. Don't feel obliged to use these; cut across the carpet to steer your own course.

Some of the more downmarket stores might put out piles of messed-up clothes, giving the impression that others have rummaged through them, as they know that some customers are reluctant to disturb a neat display, but will spend more in the store if they think they've discovered a bargain bin.

Another ploy is for shops to put all merchandise with the highest mark-up right by the entrance as they know you tend to be attracted to the first item you see when you walk through the door. Always check out goods at the back of the shop first before letting *them* make your decision for you.

Some clothing stores use what is known in the trade as a 'power display'. This is a huge, impressive show of goods, generally right inside the shop's entrance, which acts as a barrier to slow you down and get you shopping from the word go. Watch out for them.

The majority of people are right-handed and, it seems, we veer to the right when we enter a shop. Stores play on this by placing more profitable merchandise on this side of the shop – so the lesson seems to be, for value for money turn left!

Changing rooms tend to be right at the back of a shop, with high mark-up items in and around the area where you queue up. Tempting supplies will also be in all the areas where there is plenty of customer traffic – by the stairs, on the way out and around the checkouts.

Don't allow yourself to get caught up in a shopping high. When you find something fabulous, don't be tempted to buy more to go with it. Clothes might be displayed with matching accessories, while large items of furniture may be grouped with cushions or vases in the expectation that you are likely to get a buzz from spending on a bigger item and may scoop up smaller ones at the same time in your euphoria.

Ignore signs that say 'Closing-down sale, buy today'. There's no hurry – these signs can sometimes be up for months, even years, so don't be fooled. Don't be fooled either by items labelled 'deluxe' or 'premium', making you think that you're getting more for your money. Always ask what you are paying extra money for and if the shop assistant can't explain it, it's not worth it.

Men are more likely to go further into a store, which is why you often find womenswear on the ground or first floor and menswear at the back or on the second floor. And note how escalators deliver men from their own shopping area straight into women's lingerie, the place they are most likely to purchase from in a women's department!

## Get wise in supermarkets

If you are in a supermarket, use a basket instead of a trolley or use one of the smaller trolleys for food shops. A large trolley gives you the impression that you are not spending too much as it generally looks only half full and your instinct will be to fill it. A basket, on the other hand, will soon get heavy and deter you from filling it with things you don't need!

Beware of 'shuffling'. This is when supermarkets reorganise their shelves so you can never find what you want. Research shows that doing this means shoppers will visit more of the store to find what they are looking for, and will therefore look at merchandise they would not normally have come across.

Tiled floors in supermarkets are another cheap trick. The tiles in the more profitable areas of the store are smaller, which means your trolley makes its clicking noise faster and you, in turn, automatically slow down thinking you are going too fast and end up lingering where all the expensive delights are. Clever, isn't it?

Beware of end-of-aisle food displays. They usually feature things that you do not need and are not on your shopping list, but which you are tempted to pick up as you are checking out.

Most supermarkets put their most popular items and brands in the middle of the aisles so that whichever direction you're approaching them from you are likely to notice something else along that row that you were not planning on buying.

Luxury temptations can pop up in all sorts of odd places, so if you are only going into the supermarket for some bread and milk don't be surprised to find you have to walk past the confectionery counter, the flower stall and several magazine racks to get to them.

You will probably find that you are automatically attracted to a sign announcing a product and its price, and assume that you are being alerted to a bargain. Don't be fooled – often the supermarket is cleverly tempting you to buy a product that is the same price as always, but is selling slowly that week. Often, the items with these 'bargain' price signs are displayed on their own so that you can't easily compare their price with those of other brands, making you more likely simply to buy it.

Lastly, don't think that buying things in bulk guarantees a bargain. Huge packs of things are not always good value if you are not going to use them all, so think it through before you buy.

## Internet shopping

Be very careful when shopping on the Internet. Watch out for marketing ploys like, 'People who bought this book also bought ...' – who cares what other people spent their money on? Only buy what you actually need.

Offers of free postage or shipping if you spend a certain amount are likely to get you to buy something you don't need and spend more.

Don't be tempted to store your credit card details on websites. This makes it is all too easy to shop with just one click and spend before you've even registered if you need the item in question.

Remember that price comparison sites also compare prices on the Internet, not just the high street.

# The point of the Spendsmart detox

The point of the Spendsmart detox week is to begin to learn about yourself. You shouldn't worry if you didn't make it financially; you *should* worry, however, if you gathered no new information about yourself to help you change your financial outlook and behaviour for the rest of your life.

If you couldn't help but go for a splurge on Saturday night, at least you now know where your weakness lies. And you can start to think about what might be there, beneath the surface, driving you in that direction. For example, you might ask real questions about how it feels to be left out. Was there another time in your life when you felt like that? If so what have you done about it? Look at your emotional diary and use it to help you to understand. These will be vital clues that you will need as you begin to try to live life on a budget; they are the triggers that will trip you up if you're not becoming increasingly aware of them.

So don't beat yourself up. Just observe what happened, keep a note of it, and be prepared to learn from it.

# Benjamin – all in the mind

For every sale that's offered to you, someone, somewhere thinks that it's going to make them money. They know what they are doing, and the more successful the shop, the better they are at it. So, every time you agree to a transaction remember that you are pitting your wits against someone else's. It's you versus them – one of you has to get the good deal, and the other gets the bad deal.

Bear this in mind when you go out to spend. The question

you have to address is: are you going to let them get one over on you, or are *you* going to be the one to triumph over *their* efforts to take your money? Once you start to see spending as a battle, you can actually begin to prepare properly for the fight, and be more likely to triumph. As long as you know what you are up against, you have a significant degree of control over how the battle turns out. Victory shall be yours.

## Spendsmart detox – summary

Now that you've finished your Spendsmart detox week, take stock of your situation and congratulate yourself on having done something that just last month would have been unimaginable. Hopefully, you will have managed to come in just under budget and are realising that you *can* take back control of your spending, slowly but surely.

Some overspenders find that they become quite obsessive during their detox week, as they eke out their pennies, so that they have more money left at the end of it than they would ever have thought possible. This is more common than you would expect, and is proof that when overspenders reverse their habits they can make some of the best savers.

But if you blew your entire budget during the week, don't despair. The important thing is to look at your experience and try to understand why.

So now that you are feeling more in control, it's time to move on to Step Four. This is where we will put together all the information and self-knowledge you have worked so hard to assimilate, as well as where we will start to lay the foundations for a future free from money worries. It's also worth noting that the budget we are about to put together with you will most certainly not be as difficult to stick to as the last seven days on Spendsmart detox!

STEP **4** FOUR

# Spendsmart Budget

## The easy way to budget

You've made it through to Spendsmart Step Four, and this is where all your hard work is really going to pay off.

We are now going to put in place your long-term budget, and although you may have never planned one for yourself before, and may be dreading it, it's really not that bad. Having successfully completed steps one to three, you are now equipped with the necessary self-knowledge to be able to draw up a budget that you can stick to and feel positive about.

Spendsmart budgets are, quite simply, all about choices – how you choose to spend, choosing what you can do without, and what you love but might need to cut down on. It's just a question of changing your perspective on your spending, not making yourself feel in any way deprived.

Temptation is not going to disappear. If anything, the more money you have in your account, the greater the temptation will seem. But you are now more skilled at knowing how to deal with it and, most importantly, at making the right choice.

Your choice might be about getting the bus to the office or walking, while your favourite celebrity is choosing whether to fly first class to New York or get a private jet to save time – whatever the temptation and whatever the situation it all comes down to the same thing: making the right personal choice to suit your present circumstances. And it's choice that must be foremost in your mind when you are putting your budget together.

## Benjamin – staying positive

The majority of us assume that we'd have all that we needed if we had more money coming in. The irony is, that this is what everyone thinks – even the very rich. It has nothing to do with how much money we have, but everything to do with how we think about our money.

There is an assumption that rich people have everything they want. That's not true. What rich people do have is the means to buy everything that *you* want to have. If you became rich like them, you'd become aware of a whole range of other things that you'd like to have, and start fantasising about being richer still.

So the reality is that you wish you could have everything that you want right now, without the awareness of wanting anything else once you got it all. That's easy. We can take care of it right now.

Just imagine that you are the rich person who has everything that someone else wants. Who is that someone else? Perhaps someone you know who has less than you? Or someone in another country? You've got to be able to think of someone who would look at you and your life and think, 'If only I had what he or she has, then I'd be happy.' Even if you have to go to the extreme of thinking of people living in very poor conditions, you'll find that there is always someone who thinks of *you* as the 'rich' one.

So there you have it. You already have everything that *someone* wants. So you've got a choice to make. In order to have everything *you* want, you will either have to get it all, which is pointless because by the time you do you'll want more, or you'll have to want what the person who thinks you are rich wants, which is more useful.

That's really all that budgeting is about. It is your way of describing the fantasy of being rich. Construct your budget in such a way that every single item is everything that someone on this planet could want. Even if your budget is zero for something like clothes, accept that that would be perfect for someone who hates shopping and has a stuffed wardrobe already; there's always another way to look at what might initially seem like your own misfortune.

So by budgeting, you're not actually finding a way to restrict your spending. Instead you are discovering how the mind of someone who thinks you are rich works. You are describing how to think and what to want in order to believe that you have everything you could ever need. Obviously, that's not making you any richer, but it's allowing you to know what being rich *feels* like. That's what you really want, more than money, and this chapter shows you how to get it.

## Compile your own Spendsmart personal value chart

Think of budgeting as a simple way of working out what you are prepared to spend *less* on in order to have *more* money to spend on the things that really matter to you. The key to doing this is to be really honest with yourself about what matters to you and you alone. Don't just write down what you think you should spend less on. Your personal value chart should be a really useful guide for keeping you on track. It can make budgeting a lot less painful by reminding you, when you're feeling deprived, of the choices you've made in order to have enough money for things that are important to you. For example, see page 133.

## CASE STUDY

Terry seemed an oddly self-defeating sort of guy. He was running what appeared to be a successful building contracting business, except that he was always running out of money. He would blow any money that came his way, regardless of whose it was or what it was for. He wasn't getting into commercial debt, but was borrowing money consistently from his parents. He didn't use credit cards to fund his spending, but he was running into trouble. If a client gave him a deposit for a job on a Friday morning, by Monday morning it would all be gone and there would be no money there to buy the materials to do the job. Terry would then have to find new work in order to pay to do the old job, creating a situation that was spiralling out of control. He was robbing Peter to pay Paul.

While Terry's lifestyle, on the face of it, looked enjoyable, the stress of it was really getting to him. When he sought help dealing with his financial chaos, it became clear very quickly that money was literally burning a hole in his pocket. He described the feeling of having a large amount of cash on him, and how he'd be so aware of it that he felt that he needed to get rid of it.

The way Terry spent money was interesting, too. He would often spend it on other people, which made him look generous, when actually it was a case of other people helping him, because he couldn't wait to get rid of the cash.

There was something very peculiar going on. Looking beyond the surface at where these issues might have come from, it turned out that Terry was adopted at a very young age, and then had had a very hard time at school. He had had to move through a number of schools because he was dyslexic, and for much of his young life he was badly teased because the dyslexia wasn't diagnosed until he was about thirteen. He was put down by his peers and by his teachers, who told him that there was nothing he was good at, that he would never amount to anything and that he was insignificant. And one of his earliest life experiences – that of being adopted – only fuelled his feelings of being unwanted, a child who had been given away as though he had no value.

It became clear to him now that he felt literally worthless, on a very deep and painful level that was hard to talk about. Terry found it difficult to imagine being comfortable with any sense of financial worth when he himself felt so worthless. But with no money, everything made sense and it was easier for Terry to get rid of the money than to deal with the emotions he experienced when he had it.

Terry was seriously anchored to his behavioural pattern, and it was not going to be easy to help him to change. He needed to do some work both on the underlying issues and the practicalities. So he was referred to an adoption agency to begin the very difficult job of understanding how he might have felt about being given away as a child and what he might need to do about it. Given that this was a very early experience, it was really something that needed careful professional attention.

Meanwhile, on a more cognitive level, Terry was able to put together a personal value chart to help him understand his own internal sense of value, and how he would have to behave in order to reverse the messages from his childhood that told him his values were not important. His chart went something like this:

| I spend less money on | in order to have |
|---|---|
| entertaining others | money to keep my business in order |
| buying champagne | money to last longer on a night out |
| expensive home accessories such as a pool table for entertaining | a savings account to pay my tax |
| TV packages, again for entertaining | a standing order to repay debts to my parents |

# Everyone is on a budget

Don't think it is just you who is having to cut back, it's happened to most people you know. Of course we all know by now that the key to success is not about having more money to buy more things, it is about us being satisfied with what we have, but we do live in a world with rising costs and sometimes it can be a struggle to keep your head above water. Petrol prices, supermarket bills, energy costs, mobile phone tariffs, utilities bills, and interest rates are up but most of us don't have salaries that have risen alongside them. It seems having any spare cash at the end of the month to enjoy our lives the way we want is hard going so we need to think cleverly here in order to tighten your belt without feeling it, reduce your spending without becoming Nobby no friends and not take the pleasure out of buying a treat.

# THE SPENDSMART PERSONAL VALUE CHART

Consider what you are happy to spend less on, so that
you can afford the things/experiences you want the most.

### Example 1: Jay's Personal Value Chart

| I SPEND LESS MONEY ON | IN ORDER TO HAVE |
|---|---|
| Summer shoes – I wear flip-flops I buy for £20 in warmer months | More money to spend on handbags I want |
| Cars – I drive an economical VW Golf diesel as I hate flashy cars and 4 x 4s | The luxury of getting a cab when I am in town |
| Summer holidays in Europe when it's packed with kids | Winter sun somewhere exotic and quiet |
| Supermarket shopping bills, buying only what I need | More magazines I like to have as a real treat |
| Make-up and beauty items that I don't really need | A therapist come to my home for a massage |

### Example 2: Benjamin's Personal Value Chart

| I SPEND LESS MONEY ON | IN ORDER TO HAVE |
|---|---|
| Taxis which can really add up | Lunch out at work when I want |
| The latest technology | Occasional freelance admin and bookkeeping support for my work |
| Holidays in resorts or hotels | Time away with the family more often in the UK |
| Meat during the week and ready-made food | Friends over for a slap-up Sunday lunch |
| New shirts and ties | Cosy cashmere jumpers to hide them under! |

Now fill in your own:

| I SPEND LESS MONEY ON | IN ORDER TO HAVE |
|---|---|
|  |  |
|  |  |
|  |  |
|  |  |
|  |  |

## Living on your Spendsmart budget plan in the long term

First of all, it's time now to finish what we started in Step One. You will need:

- your personal debt chart (see p. 29)
- your personal spending chart (see p. 52)
- your personal value chart (above).

These three charts will arm you with the facts on which to base your long-term budget which, let's face it, you may be living on for some time, depending on how bad your debts and over-spending have been. We have waited until Step Four to do this because it's only now that you have the information and self-knowledge needed to make a realistic and viable plan. Plus, having done your detox week, you should be feeling a lot more confident about being able to survive on a budget (and remember, as promised, your long-term budget is not going to be too restrictive, just realistic).

## Forewarned is forearmed

It's now that you must remember all the lessons you've learned from previous Spendsmart steps. Only you know what you missed more than life itself during your detox week and what you hardly noticed was gone, so use these pointers to help you cut back where necessary, and go a little easier on yourself in areas where you know you find it really hard to overcome temptation. Combined with the reality listed on your personal spending chart (see p. 52), this gives you everything you need to help you fill in your new budget plan and make it one that you can really work with.

## Paying back your debts

You will also need the debt chart you compiled (see p. 29) so that you can see which debts need to be paid back first (remember – you made this priority list based on the high interest chargers being right at the top). Be aware that your creditors will be expecting you to keep the promise you made when you wrote to them in Step One saying that you'd get back to them within twenty-eight days with an offer of payment. So work out how much you can pay them back within the framework of your budget as a whole, as obviously you still need to be able to live. Once you've finalised your budget, subtract your total monthly outgoings from your income to see how much you can afford to pay back to your creditors each month.

Your debts are at the top of your budget as you really do need to prioritise them, and the list of outgoings that follows may need to be juggled around for a final budget that works.

## Repaying your debts

Your options for paying back your creditors are:

- to offer no payment for six months, after which you can review your situation
- to offer a set amount each month that you have worked out according to your budget
- to offer a nominal amount each month.

And remember:

- Don't worry if the amount you are offering to pay them back every month is small – they prefer something to nothing.
- Contact everyone to whom you owe money.
- Don't give up on trying to reach an agreement with them.
- Keep copies of all correspondence.

The National Debt helpline and the CCCS have template letters for all options on their websites (see p. 224), so don't worry if you don't know what to say. Whichever option you choose, do send a copy of your budget as creditors do look more favourably on people who they think are serious about getting out of debt.

Some payments, i.e. bills and mortgage, are non-negotiable amounts; the ones marked with an asterisk are those that you need to think about cutting back on.

Now, let's get started. Take out a pen and paper or use your computer and fill in the list opposite.

## Tips for making a budget

- Be totally honest; no more kidding yourself.
- List *everything*, however small – it all needs to be included.
- Don't be too ambitious about how little you can live on – remember this may be your budget for many years.
- Talk openly to your partner and family about how you are going to draw it up as some decisions may have a bearing on them.

# MY SPENDSMART LONG-TERM BUDGET PLAN

## My monthly outgoings

| | |
|---|---|
| Mortgage or rent | |
| Household insurance | |
| Gas and/or electricity | |
| Water | |
| Home phone* | |
| Mobile phone* | |
| Internet* | |
| TV licence | |
| Satellite TV* | |
| Council tax | |
| Car insurance* | |
| Petrol* | |
| Car tax | |
| Roadside recovery/breakdown cover, etc.* | |
| Taxis* | |
| Train fares* | |
| Private healthcare* | |
| Travel insurance* | |
| Appliance breakdown insurance* | |
| Pet insurance* | |
| Supermarket shopping* | |
| Work lunches* | |
| Eating out* | |
| Drinks out* | |
| Clothes* | |
| Toiletries* | |
| Beauty treatments/haircuts* | |
| Newspapers and magazines* | |
| Children outgoings – pocket money, childcare, babysitting, clothes, nappies, etc.* | |
| Gym memberships* | |
| Sports and hobbies* | |
| Personal fund (a monthly sum for things like glasses, Christmas, dental work, birthday presents, holidays and weekend breaks, treats) | |
| Anything else | |

MY NEW MONTHLY OUTGOINGS BUDGET IS   £

## Benjamin – who are you now?

As you prepare your budget you may feel rather remote from the subject. It's as if you are doing an abstract exercise that has nothing to do with you. If pushed, you might just be able to relate to this as something you are doing for someone else. It can be very hard to identify it as what it really is – something you are doing for yourself, and in particular for yourself to live with.

This is what's known as a reality check – when you begin to see that what you are feeling right now, as you stare at your new budget with horror, is what you've been avoiding feeling all the time you have been overspending.

We all tend to avoid some, if not most, of the reality in our lives. For example, we tend not to think much about the certainty that we will one day die. We prefer usually to think of life as very long, and therefore almost open-ended, although we know that it isn't. And the same thinking often goes with our money.

Coming to terms with your budget and accepting that it is about you and your life are a part of growing up. You are getting older, wiser, more responsible and taking control of your life. But that doesn't mean that you are getting boring or have one foot in the grave. It's actually a sign of maturity that will help you to get more out of life, not less.

You need to take this leap of faith with us because without it there is very little hope that you will be able to make any useful changes in the future based on the information that you've gathered about your past. You need a concrete plan and you need to be grown up enough to take responsibility for sticking to it. A good budget and good habits around it are the very cornerstones of getting Spendsmart.

# The Spendsmart guide to generating more money

You may be horrified when you first realise just how long it is going to take you to repay your debts, and you might want to think about ways in which to earn some extra money to get them sorted out quicker. Things like taking in a lodger for two years in order to pay back your debts in half the time; or, perhaps, taking on more work, so that you will finish paying everything off before you start trying for a baby. These may not be ideal measures, but what you must remember is that it doesn't have to be for ever. And that is really important.

## Taking on a second job

There is always work around if you want to do it, but you need to be careful about deciding what you want to do; don't take on anything that is going to require substantial amounts of money to get you started.

Think about how to make money from something you are already good at. Do you love gardening, for example, and already have the tools? If so, put a notice up in your local shops and post office, advertising garden clearing services and your hourly charges. Or, if you are a good cook, bake some cakes and cookies and sell them at work or at local Christmas fairs. Be imaginative.

TV programmes always need people for background scenes and you could spend free days being an extra and earning around £80 a day. Lots of agencies specialise in taking on extras; you will pay them commission of fifteen per cent but they do get the jobs in.

Have you got any skills you could use? Teaching children football, piano lessons or French, for example, is a great way of making some extra money. Your rates need to be in line with others in your area and your fees should be determined by just how good you are.

There are a lot of companies that use self-employed drivers to deliver their fleet cars. You need to be over twenty-five for most com-panies and you earn per job plus a set amount per mile. You are expected to fund your own way home after delivery and most want you to join up to do a minimum of one day a week, but it could keep you out of the shops on a Saturday. Contact your local auction houses and car dealers to see who is employ-ing in your area.

Babysitting and dogwalking are easy services to advertise by dropping a leaflet through local doors, but you do need to have a few skills in the area you choose. If you have children and experience of bringing up a family you could be just the type a local young mum would cherish. Walking a dog and perhaps looking after it in your home for the day can be a godsend to a busy professional who knows they are going to be working late and are worried about their pet.

Rentals are now the second most popular way of making extra income. Do you have a great car that might be popular for weddings, or musical instruments that someone might want to rent per month while they are learning? You can rent out anything from DIY tools to handbags – just use your imagination and advertise on free local sites or stick a notice up at a local school, post office or library.

Make money from shopping by being a mystery shopper. Companies employ individuals to shop, take back items, review customer service in different stores or go to a restaurant or hotel and rate the service. You don't get paid much, but you may get to keep your purchase.

These are all very easy, non-scary ways to get a little extra money in quick – which is what you need.

## CASE STUDY

Gerry's wife was in a great profession, and Gerry had, therefore, agreed to be the one to take care of the children. At first he found it was a really difficult adjustment for him to make from his previous job in a contract laundry company. He made the mistake of comforting himself with little treats here and there, geared towards making himself feel more masculine, but, in fact, getting himself into debt way beyond anything he could manage.

Gerry was determined that his wife should not find out about his overspending, so he decided to take action. At first he struggled, but after a while he got his behaviour and spending on to an even keel. He then had to address his secret debts.

Gerry was already looking after four unruly children, so he thought about how he could branch out. He took his skills from his previous job and applied them to the community of mainly mothers that he now lived in. He started a car-pool service which he organised for the whole community of mothers for a modest fee. Most of the mothers were happy to pay a few pounds a week to have someone tell them what was going to happen.

He also got into the packed-lunch business. Many of the children Gerry now came into contact with needed snacks and sometimes meals for various activities, and he found that he could provide these on top of his existing duties with little extra work.

It was Gerry's own industry and inventiveness that allowed him to get the final payment of his credit cards paid and settled. He applied his existing knowledge to a new situation and got himself out of trouble.

# Renting out a room

If you live alone and have more than one room this is the obvious – and easy – way to make some money, plus you will be splitting the bills as well which makes your living costs more reasonable.

The key to doing this successfully is to be really honest in your ad. If you love being at home and having your space, and worry about the thought of someone else on your sofa watching your favourite soap with you, you should advertise for a tenant who is out a lot, or a student who will probably spend a lot of time in their room, studying. If you live in a city you could advertise for someone who wants a weekday rent only – more and more people these days work miles away from home and only need a bed for Monday–Thursday nights.

Whoever you let to, make sure you check their references and have a proper legal document signed by both parties. This should clearly state:

- the weekly rent
- which bills the lodger is responsible for, or what percentage of the total household bills you expect them to pay
- how much notice each party needs to give to end the agreement
- the length of the agreement – usually a year or six months
- the deposit that the lodger will put down in case of damage or non-payment of rent – usually six weeks' rent in an account operated by a third party (and bear in mind that any interest earned on this amount is the lodger's, not yours).

## CASE STUDY

Bethany was the most fiercely house-proud person imaginable. She spent years making her home into her castle. But when her boyfriend left she found herself with a home that was too big for one person and a mortgage that was going up, while her income and self-esteem were going down. She was faced with choosing between losing her home or her privacy and, reluctantly, she decided to rent out her room and move into the spare room.

The money came in really handy, but at first Bethany found it extremely hard to adjust to sharing her space. After a while, though, she began to enjoy having someone else under her roof and found her lodger surprisingly unobtrusive. She valued the time that they did see each other and, eventually, her thoughts turned to renting out another room.

Bethany investigated the possibility of converting her loft, which she was able to do quite cheaply because the infrastructure was already in place. She created a suite for herself in the loft and is now a professional landlady! Her money worries have eased, she's become less afraid of sharing her space and she's made some really good friends, too.

## It pays to set up direct debits

Using direct debits means that your bills get paid on time and you won't get charged for late payments. An increasing number of companies now actually charge you *more* if you don't pay by direct debit, so this is certainly an added incentive.

## Benjamin – boundaries make us feel safe

One of the scariest possible feelings in childhood is that of feeling too powerful – that you might be able to do anything you wanted to. This might seem paradoxical, since most people's memories of childhood include the frustration of *not* being able to do whatever they wanted, and being restricted by needing the permission of adults.

But if you think about it carefully, another childhood experience is that of being somewhat out of control – learning to cope with your passion, your body, your interests, your love, your rage. All of these things require guidance and reining in. In short, young people need boundaries. They make them feel safe. It's a bit like a box in which you have room to experiment, but which you can never fall out of. Take the walls of the box away from a toddler, then he or she will be terrified about how far they might fall.

And so it is with us as adults. We never quite lose that childlike need to know where we stand. A good relationship is one in which each partner knows where they begin and end, dovetailing into one life together.

And it's the same with money, too. There's a generalised sense of dissatisfaction with the financial services industry today in that they have made credit too easy to get. We know that big financial organisations are not likely to act genuinely in our best interests and curb our excesses for us, but – in much the same way as the toddler expects boundaries to be set by adults – we do have a feeling that we'd like someone with authority to control us a little. The reality is, however, that we have to provide this for ourselves.

One of the challenges of your new budget and your commit-ment to live with it is that you will have to be the one to enforce limits on yourself. You can no longer afford to be like a child, waiting for someone to contain you, and you're not going to get away with trying to find someone else to blame. You will impose the limits, be disciplined about them and make sure that you recognise that they are in place for a good reason. These finan-cial boundaries will keep you safe and take away the temptation to act out, like a toddler having a tantrum. It's your turn be the responsible adult, so make sure when you say 'No', you mean it.

## Top Spendsmart tips for coping on a budget

For the first couple of weeks, while it's still a bit of a novelty, you may find it easy to live on your budget and stick to it. But here are some tips to make it easier to cope once temptation comes calling, as indeed it will.

- Get into the habit of only taking cash out once a week.
- If you don't see it in a shop or a magazine you can't start dreaming about it – so try to avoid shopping as a pastime or flicking through the glossies, so that you are less likely to be tempted.
- Make a rule that for every new thing that comes into your house something has to be sold or got rid of, i.e. only buy new jeans if your old ones have gone to the charity shop, only buy new food items when you have run out of something.
- Keep track of your daily spending either by writing it down or record-ing it on the computer.
- Only go shopping when you have written a list of what you need, including a note of how much you are prepared to pay for each item.

- When supermarket shopping take only enough money out with you to pay for what is on your list; leave any cards you still have at home.
- Get used to buying just one item and not automatically piling loads of things in your trolley.
- Avoid shopping with anyone who eggs you on to spend more than you need to.
- Never be tempted to hide purchases from your partner or family.
- Take things back the next day if you have made a mistake.
- Subscribe to a consumer magazine for impartial advice and information; ask around at the office or among your friends whether anyone is interested in sharing the subscription to make it cheaper.
- Choose a bank that sends text messages when you are nearing your limit.

# Children on a budget

## Jay – feeling good about giving them less

Cutting back on what you give your family can create a strong sense of inadequacy in parents. However, you should consider what taking care of a family really means: does it mean giving them everything today, with no idea of how you are going to meet their needs in the future? Or does it mean becoming more rational, teaching them to live with less, and knowing that your future – their future – is now more secure?

You will have to include your children in the budget decisions you make, but this change does not have to be a negative experience for them. Think back to when you were little, when you would raid your imagination, not your wallet, when you had to find new things to do. Explain to each of your children, in a way that is age appropriate, what a budget for the family is, and include each of them in your new way forward, so that they can learn to make their own money decisions. Encouraging your children to make choices early on in life should help them to avoid making the same money mistakes that you have made.

Get used to saying 'No', and remember that however distressed they may be at first, denying your children expensive toys and clothes is not actually child abuse. Do not give in, as by doing that you are teaching them that moaning and nagging do work in the end. Make sure you bin any shopping catalogues, as these are lethal where children are concerned, and be aware also that ads on TV will fuel their wants, too.

Give your children a set amount of pocket money at the same time each week, plus the opportunity to earn more from doing extra jobs around the house. The jobs they do and money earned for them will be dependent on what you as a family deem appropriate. You could put together charts showing who's doing what jobs and when:

## Children's rewards' chart

(Add child's name)

| Job | When? | Reward |
| --- | --- | --- |
| Putting the rubbish out | Wednesday and Saturday | £1 |
| Cleaning the car | Once a week | £2-5 |
| Washing-up/stacking the dishwasher | Every night | £1 |
| Keeping bedroom tidy | All the time | £2 per week |
| Feeding the pets | As required | £1 per week |

If you have had a big clearout and are selling some of your children's belongings, let them help you with this, then they can keep the money that their old things have raised to put towards things they might want.

Get them into the habit of swapping not shopping. There are games shops where they can swap their video games, or let them loose in your local library where they can select some great books, rather than taking them to the shops.

If you are looking for things to do in the holidays, look into free activities that you can take them to; check out what your local area has on offer, or visit websites that sell used books for guides on free days out.

Or try cooking with them at home. Buy some children's chopsticks and spend an afternoon mastering the art of sushi making. Baking's fun too – making a batch of chocolate chip cookies can usually be relied upon to lure in even the most reluctant junior cook.

Teach the children how to grow some veggies and herbs that you can use. They love to nurture plants and find it really exciting when they literally see the fruits of their labour. Go for hardy things like parsley, lettuce, carrots, potatoes, runner beans or pumpkins or, if you don't have a dedicated area for planting, use a grow bag or pots where you can still grow great garlic, sage, mint, lemongrass and coriander. If you and your kids get hooked, you might want to look into whether there is a seed exchange near you. These are meetings where people swap seeds, and where you can also get some great free advice from experts.

In summer, get out and about with picnics. Children love to help prepare for them and it's not hard to let them make sandwiches, some simple fairy cakes and a fruit salad to take out to a local park or the seaside. Or try taking them off on a fun afternoon fruit picking at a farm near to you.

Make museum trips really exciting by turning them into a treasure hunt in which they have to find clues in the pictures or exhibits as they go round. It's free, fun *and* educational!

Do use any loyalty points you may have earned from supermarket shopping to pay for children's outings. We all collect them but very few of us actually cash them in, and they can help to bring otherwise unaffordable treats within your budget.

## Benjamin – raising Spendsmart kids

Children respond well to incentives and rewards. They often enjoy being given something positive to aim for – a target to reach which corresponds to a treat of some kind.

This type of positive behaviour reinforcement system can be usefully combined with first lessons about money. If targets are reached, the child can be given some pocket money, which serves two purposes: firstly, it gives the child an awareness of the difference in value between certain items, and an understanding that more work must be done in order to acquire more expensive things; secondly, they will start to take better care of their belongings, including their money.

Kids love to learn, take on responsibility and achieve targets. Helping them do that with micro-budgets sets up great lessons for the future – that you have to work for what you want, and take care of it once you have it.

It is inevitable that when your child first has their own money, they will lose some of it and become distressed. Take this opportunity to help them understand how to take care of money they have earned. This is a lesson that may need to be taught many times, but if you persevere, they might actually get it before they reach double figures . . . which would be a considerable improvement on you!

# Day-to-day life . . . on a budget

## Car costs on a budget

Try organising a car pool system for work. Send emails out asking if anyone in the company is interested in saving money (and being more environmentally friendly) by sharing the journey to work. Americans do it all the time as they have to bulk up on numbers to drive in the special car pool lanes on the freeway so there is no reason it can't catch on here.

You could also organise a school run with local mothers, or look at cycling there with the kids in warmer months.

Find out if anyone near you is looking for cars to advertise their company/product on. You could earn quite a bit of money to put towards your car's running costs, just by having a logo slapped on to it. It does not harm the paintwork, but check how long you have to keep it on for, in case you change your mind or want to sell the car.

In big cities, car clubs are becoming increasingly popular with people who don't want to run their own cars. You just book a car, pick up one nearest to you, use your membership card to open the door, and only get billed for the actual journeys you make.

# Supermarket shopping on a budget

Talk to your family about your new budget and about how you are trying to be greener, save time and money. You now need to update the shopping list to suit everyone in the house and should ask for their input as to what they really love and what they would not miss. You may be surprised to find that the children are a bit fed up with, or may have outgrown, some of the items you regularly put in your trolley through habit. Take on board their likes and dislikes, but also get them used to making choices – yes, they can have the yoghurts they love, but not the chocolate biscuits as well. They, as well as you, need to make choices – then you can work out what you, as a family, can't live without and where it is easy to make savings.

## The Spendsmart dos and don'ts of food shopping

**Do** keep an eye out for what gets eaten and what's thrown away – is it always the same things?

**Do** keep a list on the fridge of all the things you never get around to eating, as a reminder to yourself not to buy them again.

**Do** buy supermarket own-brand products.

**Do** check out the reduced sections for bargains.

**Do** buy things that are in season; they will always be cheaper than things that are not. If you really want strawberries in November, be aware you will be paying considerably more than you would do in June, as they will be imported.

**Do** clear out a cellar, shed or dark space under the stairs to use as an old-fashioned pantry so you can make the most of buying in bulk.

**Do** buy meat on special offer. It only gets marked down when it is about to go past its sell-by date so take advantage of *safe* bargains and freeze straight away.

**Do** make a note of the quantities you need. If a recipe calls for three leeks, buy three, no more.

**Do** make use of cheap foods: rice can bulk out a chicken curry nicely; pasta with simple sauces can satisfy a hungry family; porridge is both healthy and cheap; risotto and a salad are great if you have guests, and eggs can go a long way, so make a huge meringue pavlova or bread and butter pudding for dessert.

**Do** consider cheaper options of the things you enjoy – chicken thighs instead of breasts, pork instead of beef, Cheddar instead of Gruyère – so that you still feel you are eating what you like, but doing it within budget.

**Do** try and plan your week: how many meals do you need to cook, and do you have friends coming for supper or a children's sleepover?

**Do** make a list – this is the key to food shopping budget success.

**Don't** have untidy food cupboards. It's amazing how many times we buy things we don't need, not having realised there was a full jar at the back of the cupboard.

**Don't** assume that the three-for-two offers are always a good thing.

**Don't** buy vegetables and fruit that are not sold loose – all the smart packaging costs more and is not the greenest choice either.

**Don't** buy ready meals – make your own.

**Don't** throw away leftovers – always keep anything that can make a good lunch for the next day.

**Don't** buy for a lifestyle you don't have – soya milk and bags of nuts are healthy purchases, but if you never get round to including them in your diet you're just wasting money.

**Don't** buy kitchen rolls – buy J cloths for mopping up spills, then rinse and reuse.

**Don't** buy more of something before you have actually run out, three jars in the cupboard going past their sell-by dates is a waste of money and food.

**Don't** take the kids with you – if you are stressed you will shop in a hurry and spend more.

---

## Online supermarkets

Many people find that online shopping makes their weekly bills smaller. Just log on, get what you need and search out the deals of the week. Supermarkets deliver in pre-booked slots, so you can order at work and arrange for delivery when you are home. You can also log on and compare prices from all the major supermarkets in your virtual trolley.

---

## Organic shopping on a budget

If you want to spend money on organic produce make sure you know what is worth it and why to help you prioritise your spending.

For an item to be labelled as organic produce it must have been approved by an Organic Certification Body. It means that the item has been produced by farmers who grow and process their crops without synthetic fertilisers, pesticides and herbicides, or any artificial ingredients. It also means you are buying a food that does not contain any genetically engineered ingredients. Organic producers are allowed to use up to 7 natural pesticides compared to commercial farmers who can use any of the 450 pesticides available. An organic label on meat, poultry, eggs and dairy means that it comes from animals that were given no antibiotics or growth hormones.

To help you prioritise your organic food choices, here is a list of products that are worth trying to juggle your food budget around for:

- Strawberries – as they are delicate and difficult to wash, it's worth buying organic to avoid chemicals that can stay on the fruit.
- Milk – there are no antibiotics or growth hormones in organic milk, plus it is richer in omega 3.
- Pork – non-organic pork is one of the most intensively produced meats, which means that it's most likely to contain antibiotics.
- Salads – non-organic leaves are sprayed with many artificial fertilisers as they grow low to the ground and attract insects; also, the leaves in bags of salad are washed in chlorinated water to keep them crunchy.
- Apples – the chemicals used to prevent non-organic apples from bruising or rotting in transit can be absorbed by the fruit, so washing does not get rid of them.
- Grapes and berries – these are sprayed with a high volume of herbicides, fungicides and insecticides, so it's wise to choose organic.
- Beef – organic farming standards demand that cows graze outside with only half their winter diet coming from commercial cattle feed. This means organic beef has fewer saturated fats.
- Chicken – some nutritionists advocate not touching chicken these days, unless it's free range and organic.
- Eggs – look for labels that say organic and free range; they come from hens that live healthy lives.

A lot of organic producers set up stalls at farmers' markets, so find out if there are any near you. There are also increasing numbers of companies that will deliver boxes of organic fruit and vegetables to you at home or at the office, and this can work out cheaper if you actually do use everything they send. More and more of them are now including organic meats and other produce.

## Cooking on a budget

It's amazing how many people eat ready-made meals and expensive takeaway food because they do not know how to cook. You need only master, say, ten dishes that you can freeze (chicken stew, shepherd's pie, a curry, sauces for pasta, for example) and then rotate these dishes, adding some more as and when needed. If you don't enjoy cooking you can prepare everything in one go at the weekend and put all the meals in the freezer, so that when you know you are having a night in with your partner, you can just get a curry out of the freezer before you leave home in the morning, rather than arrive home from work, realise you are both starving and spend money on a takeaway.

Ask your friends or people at work for their favourite easy weekday supper recipe – everyone has one.  Or log on to free recipe websites for inspiration – some even allow you to put in three ingredients you have in the cupboard, e.g. spaghetti, tuna and garlic, then come up with a number of recipes using those ingredients.

## Snack bills on a budget

If you were to look at how much money you spend during the day at work on snacks, you'd probably be surprised at how it all adds up. A skinny latte in the morning, a granola bar for elevenses, a mid-week lunch with your colleagues (always ends up costing more than you expected), a bar of chocolate in the afternoon, a magazine or newspaper to read on the train home . . . That's quite a bit of spending on a daily basis.

Interestingly, research shows that for many of us, it's not the coffee we're addicted to, but the takeaway cups with the lids on them. Just look and see how many adults actually take the lid off to drink their coffee. Hardly any. It seems we are all kids at heart and our caffeine-filled 'sippy' cup is what we find hard to resist!

Think about making sandwiches to take in for lunch and when you are doing your supermarket shop, buy your snacks in bulk. Why pay silly money for a chocolate bar from the kiosk at work when you can buy a multipack in your weekly shop and just pop one bar in your bag every day? As always, where your Spendsmart budget is concerned, the key to success lies not in deprivation, but in planning.

## Eating out on a budget

The important thing here is to think about places you really love going to and work out how often you can afford to eat there. Also, look at different ways of eating out, or meeting up with friends. Ask yourself:

- Is the location in question really worth the cost?
- Are there new places near by that are doing special deals?

- Would lunch work instead? Many really smart restaurants do a great lunchtime menu that costs way less than dinner.

- Or perhaps tea? A slap-up tea with sandwiches and scones at a local tearoom or hotel would cost about half of what you would pay if you were out for lunch. Plus you get a comfy chair!

If you are planning to go out for dinner, especially if it's with other people, make sure *you* take control of organising the evening. Most of us book a table for eight o'clock for dinner – something for which we pay a massive premium. Yet a lot of bigger city restaurants now do specials for tables booked before seven. This might sound too early, but think about it: you get there at 6.45 p.m., have drinks at the table, order at your leisure, probably don't start eating until 7.40 p.m. *and* pay half of what you would have paid if you'd booked the table twenty minutes later.

## Socialising on a budget

As with eating out, half the battle here is taking control. If you are going out with a group from work, do some research into places that are doing happy hours and email everyone with the time and location to meet. Organise a kitty beforehand so that you don't have to be the one to get the drinks in, and make everyone contribute. Also, don't feel you have to be out for the whole evening; stay for a few drinks, but leave before everyone heads off to an expensive restaurant you might not want to go to.

If you are going to a club with friends, plan how you are going to get there and back. Arrange a car pool and split the parking cost or ring round local taxi companies and get some quotes before you book. Never go out without planning for later – that's how you end up in an expensive minicab at two in the morning having blown your weekly budget. Plan ahead, and don't be afraid to take control and arrange things to suit yourself.

When you're going to the movies with a friend, why not catch the early bird specials – just as much fun, and you can save money too.

## Wine on a budget

For starters, check out local restaurants that let you take in your own wine – this can really make a difference. Tell your friends that you will organise the location, book the table and co-ordinate everyone, and in return they can bring the wine. Drinking something you have chosen yourselves can be a lot nicer and cheaper than settling for a cheap house wine.

If you are ordering wine in a restaurant, do ask the advice of the wine waiter and don't be afraid to say what your budget is. Be aware all restaurants mark up wine by at least 100 per cent, so it pays to know the basics in order to pay for something you are going to enjoy.

Don't feel you have to order the house wine if you don't know much about wine. Australia, South Africa, Argentina and Chile are all known to produce good value wines, so match these countries to popular grape varieties, such as Chardonnay or Sauvignon if you're drinking white wine, and Merlot or Cabernet Sauvignon if you're drinking red.

When you are buying wine for home use, buy it by the case and only go for anything that is on special offer – there is always a deal to be had in today's competitive market.

Price comparison sites are good for up-to-date information on which supermarkets or wine merchants have the best deals, as are websites with reviews of wines written by people who have actually drunk them. Sign up for emails from your local wine merchant, as they often have tasting evenings, and you can get some really useful tips from those in the know while enjoying a free glass of wine or two at the same time.

## DIY on a budget

If you want to do your own DIY work but don't have all the necessary tools, why not run off twenty or so leaflets and put them through your neighbours' doors, asking whether they would be interested in pooling their tools for communal use. All you'd need to do then would be to compile an inventory of who has which tools, along with their phone numbers, and either email or distribute hard copies of it to all those who are willing to be involved in the tool pool. This way, the next time you have a job to do around the house, simply check the list to see who has whatever it is you need, rather than going out to buy it. Plus, you might get some helpful hints or advice from someone who actually knows what they are doing!

Always sort out household repairs as soon as you notice the problem – ignoring them rarely makes them go away, and the likelihood is that they will only get worse. Check the Internet for tips on how to do simple jobs yourself like unblocking sinks and toilets, painting and wallpapering rooms and so on. Online videos demonstrating how to do just about any DIY job make many of them almost foolproof.

You might even consider joining a local evening class if you are really keen, so that you can earn extra money doing jobs for friends and relatives.

## Looking good on a budget

You don't need to have money to have style. Really stylish people know that it is better to have one amazing piece than twenty-five bargains that are not quite right, and a mix of high fashion, vintage and high street can create a far better look than a head-to-toe designer outfit. It's no coincidence that those people who look great often have stylish homes, too – it's that blend of old and new, rather than status-symbol purchases, that makes it all seem so effortlessly cool.

It's easy to shop on the high street these days without breaking the bank – even on the strictest budget – although it does mean you often end up buying quantity not quality. Clever spending, however, means knowing where your wardrobe gaps are and shopping accordingly. Your new clothing budget means buying fewer items that *really* work and less impulse 'bargains' that are never quite right. You should also allow yourself enough time to buy in a calm, controlled way, so that you make measured decisions rather than panic-buying in a spending frenzy.

Before you go out clothes shopping, take a look at what you already have in your wardrobe, and at the labels of those things you wear the most. The chances are that they come from the same three or four shops, so stick to shopping in your success stores, and become acquainted with how they work. Do they have a website where you can get good deals? When do they have their sales? Can you sign up to be informed about discount days or special offers? Get to know the sales staff at your chosen stores, and find out when they get their new deliveries, so you can get an early look-in.

Make a list of what you need to pull your wardrobe together – a blue tie, a pair of black shoes for work, some smart jeans, a great white shirt? Just write down things that you actually *need* rather than *want* and keep the list on you. Then, when you have a relapse and want to spend on something crazy but cool, refer to your list and refocus on what's important.

From now on, every time you buy a new item of clothing, ask yourself:

- Is this on my list of things I need?
- Does this fit me properly today?
- Do I have to buy other things to go with it?
- Does this solve problems or create more?

As well as shopping sensibly, learning to sew can really save you money. Get someone to show you what to do, then buy yourself a cheap mini sewing machine. You'll not only be able to repair clothes, but also give them a new lease of life.

## Ethical shopping

Shops that offer rock-bottom prices are all well and good, but they also raise some ethical issues. Many stores have come under fire because of their manufacturing practices, and all the big clothing companies are now feeling the pressure from consumers. If you do want to take advantage of cheap prices, but also buy with a clear conscience, don't be afraid to ask where the clothing was produced, whether the store has signed up to the Ethical Trading Initiative, when they are going to introduce a fair trade line or whether they already have one that you can purchase from. If they can't answer your questions think about whether you really want to spend your money there.

## Handbags

Rather than waste money trying to keep up with the latest designer must-have bag, take a look at handbag rental sites. This way, rather than buying and owning a bag that you'll have got bored with after a few months, you can hold on to the bag of your dreams for roughly the length of time that it's in fashion, and for a fraction of the price.

## Beauty

Half-used pots of products claiming to do thousands of things can be found in bathrooms the world over. Trying to work out which ones really do live up to their claims by trying them all out yourself is ultimately a mug's game, and one that you cannot afford on your new budget.

This is an area where it pays to rely on those in the know. Many of the glossy magazines publish the 'Best' lists every year, which include the best beauty buys from high-street to high-end products, as chosen by *real* experts. Make-up artists, hairdressers and industry professionals are a hard bunch to impress and they really know their stuff, so make your life simple and follow their recommendations, rather than those of someone in your local department store who is desperate to sell you something.

Websites where beauty junkies write full reviews of what has worked and what has not can also be useful and informative.

## Hair care on a budget

Don't waste money on a hairdresser unless you are confident that they understand what you want, and know what your hair type will and won't do.

It's never worth spending a fortune on a simple trim. However, if you are going for a major restyle, make sure you go to a reputable salon where the stylists cut well. Then, once you have had your hair cut in a style you are really happy with, get it trimmed every six weeks either by a junior or a less expensive professional or at an inexpensive local salon. Once a good stylist has created the lines and cut in layers, it's not hard for someone else to follow them. This way, you get a good cut and one or two cheaper trims to follow, saving plenty of money with no style loss.

The same goes for colour. A head of highlights is not cheap, so get the job done by someone who knows their stuff and make a note of the colours they use; then find out whether your local salon does training nights or find a hairdressing college near you that does, so that you can save money by letting the junior follow the pattern already created with colours that are tried and tested.

Also, look in magazines for discount vouchers – top-end hairdressing chains often do special promotions.

## Discount vouchers and freebies

Nowadays, there are a large number of websites providing details of special offers and deals in the stores. All you need to do is log on to a discount voucher site, type in the shop you are interested in, and it will tell you what, if any, deals are on at that time, along with a code word to enter at the checkout if it is an Internet store. Make it a rule to never go shopping, be it on the high street or online, without checking these voucher sites first.

Although, as a rule, it is not worth spending money on glossy magazines, other than the odd treat, they are often the bearers of discounts! Usually, these will be mentioned on the front covers, so you can find out what they are and then decide whether or not it's worth spending money on the magazine.

There are lots of websites where you can find information on freebies and giveaways. Check out sites where you can enter competitions to win anything you like from cash and clothing to holidays, computers, spa treatments and CDs.

## Swishing

Swishing – a more sophisticated version of swapping – was invented by a company that is committed to eco fabulousness and staffed by women who are passionate about saving the planet but who don't want to do it in bad clothes!

Why not host your own swishing party? All you need to swish are some fashion-conscious friends who will come over with at least one item each of clothing in really good condition that they no longer want. Make a bedroom with a decent mirror available as a changing room and get your friends to bring the drinks and nibbles in exchange for you being the hostess. Allow about an hour for everyone to have a drink while they view what is on offer, then give them the signal to make a grab for what they want. Swishing nights are great for keeping you within budget when you are just desperate for some new clothes but have no extra money. The best swish events are those where you choose a group of like-minded friends who are all roughly the same size. Or you can have a swishing evening for accessories only.

If swishing parties are not for you but you do have some clothes you don't want, check out the swapping websites.

## Fitness on a budget

Rather than pay for an expensive (and probably hardly used) gym membership, find out what local classes or fitness groups there are to get fit near you. Your local sports shop is a good place to start, as many organise running clubs or will know about groups in your area. You can also look into local 'green gyms' where you work out and do some conservation work at the same time (a double feelgood hit!). If you prefer to be indoors, check out websites where you pay for fitness videos or workout plans that you just follow in the comfort of your own home.

## Dating on a budget

You don't have to reveal your budget situation on a first date but you are going to have to think of some ways in which you can have a good time but that don't cost a fortune. Meeting for coffee rather than a meal is an easy way to start or ask your date over to your place and say you will cook for them. Think of local romantic places that you can organise a trip to – is there a great walk nearby, is there a gallery with a great exhibition on, say you are going to organise a day out and prepare a fabulous picnic, go ice skating in winter – just be imaginative and concentrate on spending time with your date not spending money. Above all be honest about your situation in a positive way. Sorting out your finances and being in a situation where you are cutting back is something to be admired not to be ashamed of.

## Entertainment on a budget

### Live TV and music

If you live in or near a city where there is a TV recording studio, find out which shows are currently being recorded. They always need audiences and it can make a really fun night out for free.

Check out if there are any free music concerts scheduled near you, as well as what your local amateur dramatics company are putting on – some of these are incredibly professional. It's also worth checking the group bookings policies on anything you want to see as quite often if you organise a group of a certain size for plays and concerts, the organiser goes for free.

Check out tour dates of bands or singers you want to see. The price difference between seeing a concert in a main city or at a smaller country venue can be huge.

## Cinema

The website of your local cinema should list details of any special deals they may be running. Don't forget to check voucher code sites as well (see p. 235), as they often have great discounts on cinema tickets. Signing up for a monthly cinema pass can often work out cheaper if you are likely to go often or take the family.

## DVDs on a budget

Most DVD players sold in the UK are 'locked', which means that you can only play DVDs bought in the UK. It is perfectly legal for you to unlock your machine and pretty easy to do. Just log on to any of the DVD unlocking sites for instructions and codes for your model, then you can buy and play DVDs from anywhere, often for about half the price.

It's worth signing up to the major DVD rental companies for special offers, you often get a free trial and prices start from a few pounds a month to rent the latest DVDs.

# Nights in on a budget . . .

## . . . for the girls

Just because you have decided to save some money does not mean that you should be having any less fun.

Why not invite some friends over for an evening of pampering? There are increasing numbers of companies that will come round to your home and do manicures, pedicures, mini-facials or tanning, and, if you can guarantee that four or five people will pay for treatments, you – as hostess – get yours for free. New designers, jewellers and even clothing stores also offer this service.

## . . . for the guys

If you can't afford to get to footie every week, you'll have work out which matches you really can't miss and budget so that you can attend them. Then, for the rest, you'll have to get used to watching the big match another way. Book your mates in advance and make match day a fun event. Ask everyone to bring something – drinks, snacks, pizza – while you provide the sofa and the TV. It may not be as exciting as being in the stands, but you do get to cheer your team on with your mates, without spending anything on travel or tickets (or blowing your budget in the pub if you had watched the match there).

You could also think about playing a sport you love, as well as just watching it. Try getting involved with a local junior football, cricket or rugby side, and get your children on board, too.

## Internet shopping on a budget

Some people find that their overspending is worse if they are buying things on the Internet. It does save time and can be great for selling (see p. 67), but it is often just *too* easy to spend – just three clicks and you get a hit. That hit, however, is over for most people the second you press the 'Pay' button, and many overspenders find that by the time the goods arrive, they don't actually want them or have even forgotten about the purchase. This is especially true of people who buy on Internet auction websites. The buzz comes from beating others to the prize or from finding that a bid has been successful, rarely from acquiring the item in question.

If you find that this is what's happening to you, *always* send these items back and get a refund if you can, or, if you are having a real problem stopping yourself, put a block on the sites/s where your weaknesses lie. Parents often use these devices to stop their children from logging on to inappropriate sites; this is no different – you are an overspender who needs to stay away from sites that cause you to break your budget, so shopping on them is as inappropriate as it gets!

## Wish lists on a budget

If you can't afford to indulge yourself, make sure you use your birthday and Christmas to really make a difference. Many people find browsing sites and putting items on to their wish lists just as much fun as shopping – the big difference is you are not paying for them. Use wish list options wherever you can so that your friends and family can log on and see what you really want as a gift and then choose something accordingly. Alternatively, ask for vouchers for shops that you know you want to spend in. And, whatever you do, don't waste this opportunity to have some treats – if you are sticking to your budget, you certainly deserve some.

# Beware of budget saboteurs

People's bank statements will always reveal items – usually consistently the same ones – that cause them problems in terms of their budget. Most of us have a spending limit over which we will mentally 'clock' specific purchases, such as a one-off expensive pair of shoes. However, forking out for two cheaper pairs of shoes in a month will often sneak in under our spending radar.

Working out where your money goes on the small things is really worth it, as it is generally the odd CD at the weekend, magazines every time you go to the shops or scratch cards whenever you stop for petrol that all add up and wreck your budget, rather than just one big spend. Figure out what your little-but-often purchases are and cut back on them. View them as treat items to indulge in occasionally, rather than as regular small spends that give you a mini-thrill at the time, but add up, consistently stretching your budget to breaking point.

## Benjamin – beating bargain-benders

How you think about the world matters, and to a certain extent your expectations of it can influence what you receive. So, if you enter every transaction with the idea that you won't, or can't, get what you want, this will have an effect on how positive you are about what you find. Conversely, if you go into every transaction with the hope and expectation of a good deal, this will help you to have a positive outlook on what you find.

This has a significant bearing on bargains. Optimists are not surprised to find bargains available. They expect it. And so they can leave it – after all, there will always be another one available when they need it. But pessimists, on the other hand, are amazed by a bargain. They tell themselves that this never happens for them, so they must take their chance before it is gone – for ever. It's the same bargain; just a different mindset.

Jumping on every bargain in case you need it, then hoarding stuff as a result, is an activity that will merely reinforce the mindset of lack. The most healthy reaction you can have to a bargain is to use it as evidence that you will always be able to find what you need and, therefore, that the world is a place of abundance. This will reinforce your positive energy around money in the knowledge that you can leave it this time, and wait for the next one if it's not something you need right now.

## Spendsmart tips for living on a budget

- Use cash not cards as much as you can. During your Spendsmart detox week you should have got used to paying for things in cash, so try to continue to use cash for everything where possible. You need to realise how easy it is to make purchases with your debit or credit cards without noticing. If you suddenly have to hand over £120 for a pair of shoes or £100 on an iPod nano and count out the tenners at the cash desk it really hits home

- Don't go to the shops because you have nothing else to do

- Don't go to the shops if you cannot stay within your budget, it may be easier not to go than to resist temptation when you are there

- Do have a goal that will keep you focused on cutting back
- Do get out a whole week's money from the cash machine in one go
- Do pay bills before the weekend, as on a Saturday there are always ways to spend money in other ways
- Don't go out to the shops without a shopping list
- Do wait a day before buying something you think you cannot live without.

## Spendsmart budget – summary

You have now completed your long-term budget, and hopefully, some of the ideas in this chapter will have helped you to look at some of the familiar everyday things you do, or want to do, in a different way. Life on a budget does not have to be a completely different life; you just need to remember that prioritising is your key, so that you still do things you love to do, only maybe not so often.

As we approach Step Five – Spendsmart Life, you should be beginning to feel more confident that you have the necessary self-control to stick to your budget, however your circumstances may change, and that's what we are going to help you with next.

STEP **5** FIVE

# Spendsmart Life

## Making the very most of your money.

In some ways, Step Five is the hardest step in the Spendsmart plan. It is certainly the one that is going to last the longest and, therefore, throw up the biggest temptations. Whatever your own personal situation in relation to money and debts, one thing is certain: things never stay the same. As we go through life, milestones such as graduating, buying a first property, having a family, career changes, needing to expand our living space, wanting to work less, all stretch our finances, and if you are on a budget you have to more careful than ever to make sure that your spending choices are right.

Make no mistake, Spendsmart life is not about giving you carte blanche to spend, spend, spend as a reward for all your efforts so far. It is a life guide covering all the areas where most of us are likely to overspend, with great ideas for how you can get the most for your money. Some tips may be obvious, while others you may never have considered, but all of them are worth thinking about and will do a lot to make your money go as far as it possibly can – which is what really matters when you are living on your long-term budget. Remember, spending money is not a problem – spending money you don't have is.

## Benjamin – get ready for a new reality

Imagine being an alcoholic. You decide to get treatment, and go into rehab. It's a great success while you are there, and you feel that you are going to be able to move on in your life and break your pattern of destructive behaviour. But then one day you have to go back to the real world. That can be daunting.

The first step might be to settle back in with friends and family. Then there will be those first few awkward moments; perhaps someone pours a glass of wine at the dinner table and looks at you for a moment, wondering if that's OK. Then a few days later a work colleague says, 'Let's go out for a drink', or you go to a bar for the first time since rehab, or a wedding, or to a nightclub full of wildly drunk people having a great time . . .

That's what you're facing now. Gradually, you have to build yourself up again to re-engage with your life – but in a different way. At every step there will be temptations and difficulties, and you'll find that you are constantly having to readjust. Nothing will come easily. You will be in familiar situations, both in terms of what is going on outside of you, and in terms of how you are feeling on the inside. Yet everything will be different. And that will feel very strange.

You will have to keep reminding yourself where you have come from – how easy it is to get into trouble by being an overspender, how far you have come in sorting out your money and how much you have learned about yourself. Would you really want to throw all that away?

Being good with money is not something you are used to, but having been an overspender, you will find it easier than most to cope in the long term. Once you switch to a new obsessive value-for-money mode, you will be able to rely on it to help you out whenever you shop. You may even find yourself getting a buzz out of saving rather than spending money. And making the most of the money you have and feeling in control of your spending is definitely something that should make you smile.

## Thrift is chic

Being on a budget means you are in good company, it has become rather trendy to not spend and to look after what you have, rather than replace it. Here is the thrift guide to what is and is not worth spending your money on, which may help you to prioritise.

| Worth spending on | Not worth spending on |
| --- | --- |
| Fresh food | Ready-made meals |
| Education | Beauty treatments and cosmetics |
| Haircuts | New furniture |
| Good shoes | New clothes |
| Investment sales bargains | Designer handbags |
| Repairs | New gadgets |
| Personal savings | Extended warranties |
| Auction room finds | Gym memberships |
| Home improvements | A new car |
| Second-hand goods | Electrical goods you don't need |

# CASE STUDY

Heather was a nurse on a very low wage, yet she seemed to have the spending habits of a millionaire – all of which were financed by borrowing more and more against her house. Gradually, she was heading for homelessness, which was not what she wanted. She loved her home – she'd spent a lot of money on it and had nowhere else to go. Yet she could not seem to stop sabotaging her finances and, therefore, her security.

Heather revealed that she had a compulsion for newness and didn't think this was odd. For her, everything had to be spotless, and as soon as anything showed the slightest sign of wear, she bought the same thing again. In her own mind, there was a rationale for every single thing she owned, yet what she revealed was a clear fear of anything becoming old or weathered – almost a fear of time.

Heather remembered being told at the age of three that her father had some kind of aneurism, and had only a short time to live. For her, particularly as the Daddy's girl of the family, this was tremendously traumatic, and it set up a dynamic that affected her life from that time on. Although she was now saying that it was a good thing that she'd been warned about her father's illness and the possibility of his imminent death, her behaviour suggested otherwise.

It became clear that Heather's need to ensure that nothing was ever less than perfect was a kind of infantile omnipotence to keep everything just the way it was. Her extreme reaction to things getting older was all about a fear of decay and the fact that time in life is limited. It makes perfect sense. If you're told as a small child that your father could die any day, then you don't want a new day, you don't want tomorrow. You want every day to be the same, over and over again.

Heather's case is a very extreme example of how loss, or in this case even the idea of loss, can really impact quite seriously on a person's mental construction about their life. Heather always came back to the idea of the house, which she didn't want to lose. It was her symbol of security, yet her whole life she lived with the threat of losing it at any minute; in the same way that she experienced the knowledge that she could lose her father at any time.

Heather was stuck in the anger phase of grief (see pp. 117–8) about her father, who actually had only recently died following a long illness, and having survived her childhood. Heather was encouraged to take some practical steps to engage with her anger and to express it. She was able to write letters to doctors whom she felt had failed the family and to express her anger safely by beating a pillow with a baseball bat. This helped her to contact her anger and once she was able to feel it and use it in a controlled way like this, she could begin to allow it to be expressed safely and therefore move on from it.

Heather had been living in a moment. She was in shock and trying to hang on to the moment. Once the feelings began to flow, she was able to move on. And she was now doing her grief work properly, instead of in the shops. Gradually, her belongings got older and her finances got back into shape. By articulating and getting in touch with that missing phase of her grief process she was able to move quite quickly back into a much more normal frame of mind and relationship with her finances.

Heather's story is a perfect example of how a change in attitude to money may necessitate a proper examination of where that attitude comes from in the first place. Sometimes will power alone is not enough.

# Spendsmart tips for shopping in sales

The sales can be a good time for you to replace wardrobe staples or to buy items of furniture you wouldn't be able to afford at regular prices. Here are some tips for sales shopping.

- Make sure you know when a sale is going to start and what the discounts are going to be. Sales staff will know a couple of days before the sale what is going to be reduced and by how much, so don't be afraid to ask. Some stores even have sale previews, so you can see what is going in the sale. These items are also featured on the stores' websites.
- Get there early for the pick of the bargains.
- Once a sale has begun, don't be afraid to ask staff when the second mark-downs will be – usually two or three weeks after the sale begins – as further discounts can make a big difference, and if there is plenty of stock you are unlikely to miss out. If, however, the item you're interested in is the last one, then it is a question of holding your nerve to get a better deal.
- Go to furniture shops with a tape measure the day before their sales begin, so you can work out which items are right for your home and make calm decisions the evening before the sale, rather than panic-buying and finding that what you have bought does not fit into your house. Don't forget to measure doorways and halls at home too.
- Be aware that many shops alter their returns policies during a sale, so don't make assumptions – check before you buy.
- Always ask yourself if you would be prepared to pay full price for any item you're interested in buying.
- If you want to buy a sale item on an Internet site, remember that the sale starts at one minute past midnight on the date in question. (And bear in mind that if the site is a European- or USA-based one you'll need to take into account any time differences.)
- If you know what you want then the first choice is where to get it. The Internet is a great tool for being able to compare prices.

- If your 'can't live without' clothing items are on sale then this is a good time to stock up. Go for things like cashmere or good shoes that you could not afford if they were not on sale. For clothing and home look for classics in neutral colours, not the acid green on sale because no one but you is prepared to pay for it.
- Wear good underwear when sale shopping for clothes, as you will probably have to change in a communal changing room if the sale is busy. Wear clothes that are easy to take off, as you never want to buy something without trying it on first.

## Your home

This is where you live and spend much of your time, so it should be a welcoming place that reflects your lifestyle and personality. The best homes to be in are those that are filled with things that really mean something to their owners, not those that are packed with the latest must-have furniture statements.

It takes time to build a house into a home that you love, and you may have to live somewhere for a while before you achieve the look you really want given limitations of space and cost. Whatever your budget, you can have a great home if you just take your time over making decisions – being on a budget does mean that every purchase counts.

## Benjamin – house or home?

Home means so much more than just a house. It's a deeply evocative word that creates all sorts of associations for all of us. We often express ourselves very deeply within our home; in the home that we choose and the way that we live in it. We are all, perhaps, conscious that our home reflects in some way a part of ourselves. So, as much as we are interested in the general project of improving ourselves and our lives, we are also interested in the specific project of improving our homes.

The problem is that we can get carried away, and not be aware that we are doing it for the wrong reasons. Sometimes, a compulsion to have the perfect home at any cost can be covering up disquiet in other areas in your life – in your relationship or with your family. When you just have to have something for the home, or there's some improvement that you can't bear to do without, you must stop for a moment and think about whether or not it is really necessary in terms of your domestic environment, or whether it might be a distraction from other tensions or problems.

The home is also a very visible presentation to others of who we are. Sometimes we can become very other-centric, meaning that we run our lives on the basis of what we imagine others might be thinking. So we present our homes in such a way that we think will win their approval, even if it is not what we like ourselves. This can mean that we end up losing sight of what we want, and who we really are.

So we need to think more carefully about what we want from a home and why.

First of all, imagine that there was no one else in the world but you and the people you live with. Would that change the way that in which you organise and present your home? You'll have to work quite hard to think yourself into a world in which no one else exists, then figure out how you want your home to be. Is it different from what you thought you wanted?

Next, consider your relationships with the people you live with. Are there things that you feel you can't say to them? Things you wish they would do? Things that you've never asked for from them but which you think would change the dynamic of your living arrangements if you could? Make a list of these things and imagine then saying, and asking, for them all. Now think about your home and what you want from it physically. Is it different now? Is it less? Does it seem less important? This may tell you where the real home improvements need to be done.

## Don't move – improve

Before you consider estate agents' fees and other moving costs, take some time to explore what you have already got to ensure that you are using your space as efficiently as possible – most of us don't. You may need to get independent advice on how to maximise the space you have, as it can be hard to stand back and see your home in a dispassionate way. Visit websites for free inspiration.

## Utilise all your spare space

If you feel you are bursting out of your home, think about whether you are using every inch of available storage space. Think about the space under every stair and put shelves higher up so you can fit more in. If store shelving ranges don't fit, get custom-made MDF shelves which can work out cheap and get a local carpenter to put them up for you.

If you have built-in cupboards, try wallpapering or painting them to blend in with your room, or line the wall behind shelves with mirrors to make a small space look bigger.

Do make sure you use the space above your wardrobe rail – you can buy rails that pull down, for extra hanging, and buy some inexpensive under-bed drawers that make putting things away no hassle.

Put up hooks on the backs of your doors, especially where you are stuck for space in bedrooms and bathrooms. Cubed storage cupboards above the lavatory or above your headboard are also great for utilising dead space.

In kids' rooms, look at loft beds that can house a desk and mini-wardrobe underneath them.

Make false walls by applying plasterboard to a timber frame attached to existing walls, and use them to house recessed shelves. These can also hide cisterns in a bathroom, and are great behind a bedhead to create storage. Investigate whether you can put storage under your floorboards and, if so, put in trapdoors so wine and tools can be stored easily. Make the most of wall space in downstairs bathrooms, up the stairs or above doors to house books and CDs.

## Extensions

Extending your space is undoubtedly cheaper than moving, but remember the golden rule of extensions: the cheapest option is to knock down an internal wall, next it is going outwards with an extension, then it's upwards for a loft conversion or another floor. The most expensive option is digging down to create a basement. Don't enter into any of these without getting at least three quotes from builders who can supply references!

## Budget home buys

Sometimes it can be better to buy one large piece of furniture if you want to make a room look bigger, rather than several smaller ones, especially to keep rooms clutter-free.

Don't be tempted to buy into the latest trends; stick with things that you really like and that suit both your personality and your home. Whether it is contemporary, oriental, shabby chic or just white and simple, know your own style and don't spend money on things that don't fit in.

Buy in groups. Three smaller hanging lights can work out cheaper than one big statement one, and bookcases, likewise, are often far cheaper for the smaller models that can then be stacked.

Buy things that work in both winter and summer, i.e. a great hurricane lamp with a simple chunky church candle in it can have sand added for the summer and just put fresh cranberries à la Ralph Lauren around it for winter.

Spend money on things that get more attention: our eyes naturally go up, not down, so prioritise on that basis.

Look out for designer diffusion ranges. Top designers now do great lines for many department stores and you can get their brilliantly designed pieces at great rates.

## Shelving

Good safe economy buys are the floating shelves or sets of boxes and blocks which can be mixed up depending on what you want to store in them. Think about what you are going to store before you buy, making sure they will accommodate taller files or a heavy music system, for example. As a general rule 1 metre of shelf supports 5 kg in weight.

## Walls

Paint walls in neutral colours and use accessories like throws, blankets, candles and cushions to change the mood – it's cheaper and more fun. When choosing paint colours, try out sample pots of more expensive paints, then copy them with mixes of more reasonable ones. Always paint walls with a hardener so that you don't mark them, especially if there are kids around.

If there is a designer wallpaper you really love, but can't afford to buy enough of it to do the whole room, think about making a feature of just one wall. The walls behind beds or fireplaces are good ones to choose. You can easily get ends of rolls from designers and, if your budget will only stretch to a little paper, you could always paste it onto a canvas and hang it up or use it to customise furniture. A funky wallpaper can also look great in the panelling of doors, or under the glass on a coffee or dressing table.

If you have a favourite print or large photograph, try having it enlarged to poster size or turned into a canvas to decorate your walls. You can even find companies that will blow up a picture to cover a whole wall. It's also worth taking a look at local students' shows for affordable art.

Big wall spaces like halls can be filled with arrangements of framed photographs grouped together in themes. Frames placed vertically in a row work well in a narrow space as it draws the eye upwards, while larger pieces in a horizontal row can help to widen a smaller space; position the most important one in the middle and work outwards. Find inexpensive frames in the high-street shops or check out websites that do words, phrases, initials or whatever you like in kits that you can stick to the walls without damaging them.

Look at using wall stickers. They are great if you change your mind a lot and are self-adhesive and removable. Choose from Damien Hirst-style dots or have a phrase or well-known saying turned into a graphic to put up.

## Flooring

To save money here, buy carpet, tiles or wood flooring in the sales, but save on the flooring itself, not on the laying of it, which can be tricky and calls for a professional.

Bear in mind that real wood needs a lot of maintenance, so if you are unlikely to keep this up, choose a wood effect that looks like the real thing, but cannot be damaged by furniture or high heels. When choosing, remember that darker colours like walnut and American maple will make a room look smaller, while paler ones like beech, maple or oak will make it look more spacious.

## Bedrooms

Take tips from hotels and make the mood in your bedroom calm. Buy the biggest bed your room will take; lower ones are easier to step around if your bedroom is small. When money is tight, spend more on the mattress and less on the frame to ensure comfort on a budget.

Declutter bedrooms by making use of all available space (see pp. 180–1).

When it comes to bed linen, the nicest and most hard-wearing is either 100 per cent cotton or linen. Ask for expensive sets as a wedding present or big birthday gift, or buy yourself 100 per cent cotton in the sales.

When you're choosing mirrors, the purchasing rule here is the bigger the better. Check out prices at your local glass shop where they can cut a mirror to the size you want. If your bedroom has either a crooked ceiling or asymmetrical walls, an oval-shaped mirror can help to disguise this.

Use any spare space behind the bedhead by putting up a screen and getting some extra storage space. Also buy inexpensive under-bed drawers to declutter, which can be cheaper than a wardrobe or chest of drawers.

## Living rooms

Go for blinds rather than expensive curtains. American-style shutters are great and if you take the time to measure your windows up properly and choose the ready-made ones, they can be quite reasonably priced. Alternatively, look out for simple wooden blinds that can really brighten and open up a room.

Choose the biggest sofa you can without it overwhelming the room. Metal legs look more modern than a traditional skirt. As a general rule, a small room can take a sofa of up to around 1.8 m in length, while a larger room can take 2.4 m.

Always sit on a sofa before you buy it; some modern designs look cool but are really uncomfortable. Choose a plain fabric that will not date and get it protected so that it won't stain too easily. You can also buy loose covers, so if there's a stain that is ruining the look of your sofa, and your budget won't run to a new one, you can still disguise it.

Dress up a cheap coffee table by taking the clear glass top to a local glass shop and getting them to cut the same size in mirrored glass. The new surface will look modern and give the room an updated feel.

Don't waste money on storage containers – keep shoe and gift boxes and cover them in wallpaper or wrapping paper to store adaptors, leads, camera stuff, buttons, keys, and so on, rather than buying expensive storage boxes.

Look for furniture that you can move around. Modular furniture can divide a room and can be used in loads of ways. Get one large piece of furniture with shelving of different sizes to stack your TV, DVD player, CDs and books.

## Flowers

Cut flowers can work out really expensive, so try using bulbs or plants instead. Fill glass vases with earth, plant hyacinths, daffodils, orchids, or hydrangeas and place moss on the top for a professional finished look (you can get this from the garden centre). This also works well with sand or white gravel, depending on the plants. Or put individual plants in smaller pots and line them up on a mantelpiece or table. They can last for up to three weeks and work out at about a third of the price of a bunch of flowers.

## Dining rooms

Modern living spaces often do away with formal dining rooms, doubling up eating spaces as studies. If this is the case in your home, look for chairs and tables that can fold up easily and be stored out of the way so you can use the space for other things.

Change your china rather than changing all the furniture to get a new look, go for bright colours or different shapes to jazz things up.

## Kitchens

It's so easy to overspend in the kitchen, but it is not necessary. If your existing built-in cupboards are showing signs of wear and tear, why not paint them or think about replacing the doors only. Even expensive kitchens have the same basic shell behind the designer doors, so it's rarely worth replacing the casings. Just changing the handles on a simple door can make a massive difference.

You can also achieve a new look for less in the kitchen by replacing the worktop surfaces. Look up your local stonemason and check if they have any end-of-line offers and buy it 5 cm thick to make it look more expensive.

## Bathrooms

Choose clear not frosted glass for shower screens to help make a small room look bigger. Glass is not expensive, so get a quote from your local glass company to cut huge pieces of mirrors for a whole wall, rather than buying expensive tiles. You could also use wall-paper and put plain glass over the top to protect from splashes.

Don't spend money on expensive blinds that will get water damaged – just use something on the glass instead. You can buy cans of frosted glass spray (although applying it does require a steady hand) or frosted film that you simply stick on to your window.

## Home offices/studies

Working from home does not have to mean investing in a huge great desk, computer and all the trimmings. If you buy a small, modern laptop and compact printer, you won't need a huge, expensive desk to accommodate them. Buying office supplies can really add up, so try and buy in larger quantities, or add your order on to your company's to benefit from the best prices (no stealing from the company's stationery cupboard please). For cheap ink cartridges, enter the number of your printer in a search engine to find out about companies who will refill your empty ones.

## Gardens

If you are not a keen gardener don't waste money on high-maintenance plants. Look for hardy perennials, perhaps a few easy-to-grow vegetables, and use the rest of your garden budget on decking and shrubs and nothing else. Gardeners are gener-ous with their time so ask them for advice on what is worth buying and do shop around online to compare prices if this is a world that is new to you. If you really want to keep maintenance down, just go for gravel borders and clean lines for a modern Zen look.

## Auction houses

Do make sure you visit your local auction house to check out what they have to offer. Many have a huge range of traditional and contemporary furniture for much less than it would cost to buy in the shops. Staff at the auction house will be happy to explain to you how their bidding system works, if you are not familiar with it, or you can go and visit an auction the week before you want to buy and see the process in action.

# Your wardrobe

A lot of us spend money on clothes because of poor body image. We all have something about ourselves that we don't like and shopping to improve our self-esteem is a familiar overspending habit. The key to breaking this cycle is to be honest and realistic about your body and to shop for that reality, not for the fantasy.

Stand in front of a mirror and take a good look at your body. Then give yourself marks out of ten for each body part – legs, hips, bum, stomach, arms, shoulders, ankles, and so on. Now look at your answers; the lower the number the worse your body image is for that part, but while you might give every part a low mark, there will be some that you hate less than others. If you can be honest about your body reality, future clothes spending will be so much easier. The golden rule here is to spend more on disguising the parts you hate, and less on the parts you like.

Ask friends for their old magazines and compile your own style file by tearing out anything that you like: the cut of a jacket, the heel on a shoe, whatever you fancy – just flick through and tear out. After a few weeks, you should end up with about thirty to forty tear sheets – enough to spot trends and details that consistently catch your eye. This is key, as it shows what you are truly drawn to, and will mean that you start buying things that you instinctively like, rather than being swayed by marketing or celebrity endorsements.

So, remember the golden spending rule: more on the bits you hate, less on the bits you love. If your bum is huge, buy a really well-cut expensive pair of trousers to minimise it, and spend less on a great top to team them with. If you are a guy with short legs, buy a cheaper shirt and a pair of flattering jeans to minimise the defect.

Don't just wear black – anyone can wear colour. Think of your body as being divided at the waist and wear brighter or difficult colours that don't suit your hair or skin tone on your bottom half. Blue may be a disaster next to your face, but a great cobalt skirt or a pair of navy trousers with a subtle top could really work. Remember also that khaki and denim are neutral, like black, and will go with everything without looking quite so hard.

If you are tempted to spend more than you usually do on an item think about how useful it is going to be. Ask yourself the following four questions:

- Can I wear it in the summer?
- Can I wear it in the winter?
- Can I wear it in the day?
- Can I wear it in the evening?

If it gets any less than three out of four ticks, it is not worth big money.

# Benjamin – Cinderella story

The original fairy tale of Cinderella's transformation from slave to princess is one of the most deeply rooted stories in our culture. It strikes at the heart of a fantasy that a young woman's life, typified by powerlessness and drudgery, can be transformed by the touch of a suitable man's hand.

The idea that a whole life transformation can happen, literally overnight, is a very powerful and seductive one. After all, there are usually so many things that we'd like to change about our lives. Certainly, most of us would like to be richer, but then there are other things, too – we'd like to be better looking, more respected, in a good relationship, in an important position with a purpose in life. All of these are embodied by the imaginary transformation into a princess. And all it takes is one willing prince.

In the original story, Cinderella's chance for this desirable introduction hinges upon an invitation to the palace ball, for which, if she is to attend it, she needs a suitable dress. And that's where the trouble starts, because today, we (and women in particular) often apply this fairy tale to ourselves in real life. The thinking tends to be: I'm not happy with who I am, but a relationship with a great man could fix that, so I'm going to have to find the perfect outfit so that he'll want me. Job done.

The way in which people do nowadays rise from obscurity to celebrity status, seemingly from one day to the next, has fuelled this fantasy, so that it actually seems reasonable to expect that someone with neither talent nor good looks can become rich and famous. Not so long ago, many of us would lap up images of people like Jackie Onassis or Princess Diana, but few people ever thought they could be them, or even be like them. Today, however, everyone thinks they can be a Victoria Beckham. After all, she did it, so why not?

The problem is that the story of Cinderella is an allegory. It is mythical in structure, which is the real reason why it resonates so deeply with us and especially with women. Cinderella herself represents everything that is kind and virtuous about the female psyche. The ugly sisters represent everything that is venal and capricious. So the story is really about the magical triumph of virtue over greed. Only the point is that the magic is internal. In the real world, most people have both good *and* bad sides to their personalities, and what the story teaches us is that if we work on ourselves to create a beautiful inner world (as represented by the various items given to Cinderella by the fairy godmother), at some point this will be manifested in a better reality around us. Work on your internal reality and sort out your inner problems, and you will forge the path to lasting change in your external circumstances.

So it is that shoppers who focus so intently on getting the 'right' look are setting themselves up for a time-limited high, because at midnight the clock will always strike and the clothes or accessories that seemed so magical at the time of purchase will become commonplace. Real, lasting change begins on the inside, then works its way out, happily ever after . . .

## Outlet stores

Outlet shopping is a good way to shop in reasonably smart surroundings, with good discounts and customer service. The reductions are usually 50 per cent or more and the best time to hit these stores is usually early spring or early autumn, just after the traditional sales periods when they are likely to receive their biggest deliveries.

## Shop the world

Spend more time researching via the Internet, and this will mean, ultimately, less time on bad spending. Sign up with a company that gives you your own P.O. box in the USA so you can shop on the American websites that won't send abroad, as they consistently offer great savings. Don't forget to factor in boring customs duties, however.

## Vintage and second-hand clothes shopping

The trick to buying vintage clothing is making sure you know how much things are worth. Don't think that vintage automatically makes things cheaper, the prices can be affected by what is in at the time and if it is a popular designer item it may still cost more than you want to spend.

Buying vintage can be a really good way of buying quality as many of the older pieces will be extremely well made. You do need to do some checks before you buy, however, as many shops or markets won't take things back.

Make sure you go with someone else as there may be a shortage of changing rooms and mirrors, so you could probably do with a second opinion on how things look. And never go by the size on the label – older sizes vary wildly, so always try things on.

Set aside more time for vintage shopping than you do for high-street shopping, the hit rate is lower, but worth it when you get a bargain.

If you are buying jackets, look inside at the seam under the arms, this is the area that is going to go first. Check for any stains in a good light and don't be afraid to haggle over the price. Vintage clothing will probably need to be dry cleaned rather than machine washed due to its delicate nature, so factor that in to your cost. Also, bear in mind that many stains cannot be removed, so don't buy something that is badly stained thinking that you'll be able to sort it out with a modern stain remover. Most vintage clothes need careful handwashing, so don't ruin them in a washing machine, and never tumble-dry them.

## Vintage shops

Don't expect don't these shops to be laid out neatly like a high-street store. Prices vary and there are bargains to be had, but you might have to rummage around to find them.

## Vintage clothing fairs

These are great places to find a bargain as you get lots of sellers all under one roof. You usually have to pay an entrance fee to get in, so go at the end of the day for bargains and remember to take cash.

## Car boot sales

You never know what you are going to find at these and regulars say the best booty is to be found outside of city centres. Do take cash to pay.

## Markets

Check out listings for antiques markets and fairs and also find out whether any are happening wherever you happen to be on holiday. There are some great flea markets in Europe and also in the USA – the one at the Rose Bowl in LA is legendary. Usually, there are some great stalls at these markets, but an awful lot of rubbish too, so it does take time.

## Charity shops

These can be great places to shop, and are generally really cheap. Plus, you feel good helping a charity, too. A good trick is to go to the branches in more upmarket areas where wealthy locals unload their cast-offs. Increasingly, charity shops are starting to sell furniture as well, and many charities are teaming up with designers and displaying their items at fashion events and music festivals.

### Vintage shopping on the Internet

Vintage clothes sites are growing and with the eco trend for swapping, rather than buying new things, many are expanding really quickly. You will find most of the mainstream sellers on eBay, but do ask them for actual sizes of their pieces, and whether you can return anything that does not fit.

# Beauty

A top make-up artist once said that it's better to spend more on products that go directly onto your skin and less on those that go on lashes and lips. This is not a bad way to save money, and here are some more tips:

- Look for products that do more than one job – a blusher and bronzer in one, a moisturiser that contains sunscreen, a stain for lips and cheeks.
- Go cheap on trend buys – metallic eye shadows, the 'in' colour nail varnish; chances are that you will get fed up with these before you use them up, so don't spend much on them.
- Go for cult cheaper bestsellers like Maybelline mascaras.
- Don't spend a lot on expensive eyeliner and eyebrow pencils – the difference in quality is not enough to justify the price. Pressed powders are also pretty much the same across the board.
- Never have too many products on the go at one time as they go off much quicker than you would think.

- If you are thinking of having your teeth whitened, don't go to a pricey salon. There are plenty of inexpensive whiteners on the market, but ask your dentist for advice before doing anything.
- Whenever possible, buy beauty products abroad; all the French makes are obviously cheaper in France, as are the American big names in the States.

## Contact lenses and glasses

Go to your optician and ask them for your prescription. You are perfectly entitled to do this, and it means you are then free to shop around for good deals. You can save up to 50 per cent buying contact lenses online and an enormous amount on glasses too.

Also, remember to take your prescription with you on holiday, as prices for both sunglasses and regular glasses can be much cheaper in places such as Singapore, Bangkok and the USA.

## Children's parties

Children love a party, but not necessarily in the way that we might imagine. They're not that bothered about the expense; what they want is the freedom to have as much fun as possible.

Be brave enough to strike a balance between what you provide and leaving enough room for the kids to express themselves. You don't have to use an expensive entertainer, but you do need someone to be in charge. Buying a piñata for the garden and getting them all to attack it with sticks is a good way to keep them occupied, as are traditional party and dancing games. They are with their friends and will have fun regardless of how much the party has cost you.

If you have enough space to give a party at home, then do. Renting venues is expensive. Don't feel you have to invite all the children in the class, depending on your child's age it can be overwhelming.

As far as food is concerned, children love party food, so don't be tempted to spend on things they won't eat. Stick to traditional sandwiches on wholemeal bread, chocolate crispy cakes and some veggies and dips, with jelly and ice cream for dessert and, of course, birthday cake. And don't spend a fortune on going-home bags either – a few little treats is all that's necessary.

If you want someone else to take total charge then think of a theme that will suit and go for it. Baking parties, pizza parties, make-up parties, pet parties, chocolate parties with chocolate fountains, it's up to you – just pick something relevant to the size of the group and their ages and watch them love it all.

## Adults' parties

Do send out invitations – nothing expensive, just something to give people an idea of the sort of party you are hosting. Invitations are also useful in that people are less likely to bring a friend or friends along to something that looks more formal, making it easier for you to control the numbers. Keep a regular check on the numbers so that you don't end up over-catering – you cannot afford to underestimate the drop-out rate.

The drink is probably going to be your biggest expense if you are planning on having a party at home, so be aware of what is good value and what is not. Check out online deals as buying in bulk can mean good savings. Your best bet is to do a couple of cocktails (or Pimm's if it's summer), which means your drinks will go further than if you were to give everyone just wine or beer. Buck's Fizz is a popular option (orange juice with champagne or cava; or use lychee, mandarin or mango juice instead). Ask friends to bring a bottle of whatever spirit you are using for your cocktails – most people would love to be told what you want, rather than trying to second-guess you.

It is easy to do your own canapés – a choice of five types is about right, and you need to work on the basis of roughly ten pieces per head. Easy and cost-effective suggestions are:

- small sausages cooked with honey and mustard seeds; pick decent chipolatas otherwise there will just be loads of fat and very little sausage
- tricolour kebabs – half a cherry tomato, a basil leaf and a cube of mozzarella all skewered onto a cocktail stick
- small blinis topped with crème fraîche and a tiny sliver of salmon
- melba toasts with home-made pâté
- bruschettas – toast ciabatta squares, rub with a garlic glove and pile grilled vegetables on top (red, yellow and orange peppers look good), or buy some tapenade and spread it on
- marinated chicken breasts on sticks – marinate in garlic, herbs, chilli and soy sauce before cooking, then cut into bite-sized pieces
- strawberries, pineapple chunks, grapes, and marshmallows dipped in chocolate and served on sticks.

If you can't afford to do food, specify on your invitation that you are hosting drinks. If you clearly state 'Drinks from 7 to 9 p.m.' on the invitation, people will understand. And, if it is around Christmas, many people will be doing two parties in a night, so it won't be a problem at all.

Grab some flaming torches or plain church candles (depending on the season), and you're all set!

# Weddings

Weddings can be a huge expense and the source of enormous hassle and pressure, but it does not need to be that way. You can do a wedding beautifully on a budget without having to feel you've been cheated.

To keep costs down choose one theme only and stick to it. Sit down with your partner and talk to them about what the most important things are for you both. Your partner might want two hundred people at the reception, while you would prefer only eighty so that you can afford an expensive dress. Whatever it is be really honest with each other, as if you don't do it before the serious planning gets under way, someone is going to feel resentful on the day.

Allocate your money where you really want it to be. Would you rather spend it on the wedding lunch, or on a memorable honeymoon? It's all about choices, and on a budget it is crucial to make the right one.

## Benjamin – on weddings

Weddings are a bit like homes in that they represent something important about who we are, and who we wished we were; and we never quite know who they are for. But unlike our homes, weddings are brief and without lasting tangible value. They serve no purpose in the material management of our lives, nor do they constitute a lasting investment. In that sense, they are froth; they are the icing on the cake of love and romance, not the cake itself.

All too often a wedding is seen as a status symbol, or something to keep others happy – an affair in which the quiet act of marriage betrothal is shouted down by the roar of the wedding process. Within the madness and the mayhem are two people choosing a lifelong and singular commitment to love and cherish each other. But this point of focus gets lost, to the extent that people nowadays often arrive at their own weddings on the verge of a nervous breakdown, while their guests might experience a nonchalant sense of déjà vu, as they take in the marquee, the salmon starter, the three-tier cake and the two-tier table hierarchy.

Somewhere along the line, agreeing to be married and getting married become two different things that are very distinct from one another. What separates and changes one into the other is the wedding.

A wedding, therefore, has to focus on the importance of these smaller acts of intent. It must not become so big and so hectic that the moment it is designed to celebrate gets lost. So, instead of letting a social whirl or fashion statement lead you into the service, mark the day with the simplest act of all; a choice deep in your heart to commit your life to a fundamental change. Once you have that sorted as your priority, all other decisions will become incidental and much easier to make. And if, at any point, you find yourself awash with choices, return to that place. Hold it tight and make all of your decisions from the secure position of that fundamental one of voluntary union.

## Rings

You don't have to spend a fortune on wedding and engagement rings. If you don't know much about jewellery, the main thing to remember is that you will pay more for bigger stones, so you'll get more for your money if you choose a design with pavé diamonds (little tiny chips that really glitter). There are fabulous diamonds at about half the UK price in Bangkok, Dubai and Antwerp if you happen to be nearby at any point. Also, if you are visiting the USA, book a trip to either New York's or Los Angeles' thriving jewellery districts that give excellent value for money. The savings may well mean that you can take a weekend trip to the USA to propose! Nowadays it's safe to buy diamonds on the Internet: many sites offer money back and full certification guarantees.

## Venues

Many venues have different prices for different times of the year, so if your heart is set on a particular venue, but it is out of your price range, you might be able to get around this by being flexible with your date. Try asking about prices in November as this is often the cheapest month.

Think about how you make a basic space look fabulous. Contact local prop houses, or TV studios. Eight enormous chandeliers hung low with candles, ribbon, holly or whatever you fancy can make a really bold statement. Ask garden centres if they will hire out large trees for the day, then disguise the tubs with pretty fabric or paper and thread fairy lights through the branches. This can transform a room, and for very little money. The golden rule here is to think big – tall trees, huge candles, loads of tealights or enormous glass bowls with floating candles all work wonders.

If you've spent less for a modest venue, it's worth spending a little more on great lighting and decorating the walls. Giant letters spelling out words like 'Love' or the date of the wedding or both of your initals across a big wall can be very effective.

Just make sure that they can be removed at the end of the day without causing any damage.

When you call to check out a venue, don't mention the word wedding! Tell them that you are booking for a party, as some venues charge up to 30 per cent extra for weddings. Go for places where you are allowed to take in your own alcohol and where crockery, cutlery and glassware are included in the price.

Prices are often reduced for receptions or lunches that end during the day. (Also, you find that people eat and drink less at that time than at evening dos.)

Visit your local village hall – kitsch can be a cute way to do a wedding, if you get it right. Think bunting, tables groaning with old-fashioned home-made tea delights, retro tablecloths and flowers from the garden. It's inexpensive and means that you can put more money into something else.

If you are going for a marquee, know where to spend your money. Big white tents need the right lighting, so factor that into your budget. Check out the marquee company websites for free inspiration too.

## Invitations

American websites are great for inspiration and keen prices on the invitations front. Choose flat or laser printing as it is cheaper, or go for custom-designed postcards. Don't waste money on save-the-date cards; just get your invitations out early so that people have plenty of advance notice. And don't send expensive RSVP cards either. Nowadays, couples set up a website where people can email their replies.

Another idea for cutting costs on invitations is to buy a personalised embosser or stamp to create an expensive look at a really low cost.

## Dresses and suits

Renting is definitely the best option for the groom. As for the bride, remember that you will only wear your wedding dress once and that any plans you might have for dying it and wearing it to parties after the big day just won't happen. If you are getting married at a registry office, think about getting a great dress in slate, caramel or a soft light grey that you can easily wear again.

If, however, your heart is set on a white dress, check out stores that do evening dresses that would work for a wedding and choose extra-special accessories to give it that bridal look. Alternatively, you could choose some material at a local fabric store and ask a dressmaker to copy something you have seen and love. Or, think about cutting back on an expensive veil and shoes in order to have the dress you want.

Designer bridal shops do have annual sample sales with up to 75 per cent off, so check when these are well in advance of your big day if you have fallen in love with a Vera Wang!

## Bridesmaids and ushers

Don't think you have to give expensive gifts to your bridesmaids, best man and ushers. Most people are just thrilled to be asked and do not expect anything else.

If you let the bridesmaids choose dresses they like and would wear again, they will probably be happy to pay for them themselves. But if *you* insist on jamming them into lemon chiffon, you have only yourself to blame when they insist *you* pick up the bill!

## Flowers

Find the nearest wholesalers' market to you that is open to the public and have a good look around to see what you like, bearing in mind that flowers that are in season are always the cheapest.

In spring that means narcissi, hyacinths and daffodils by the armful – either in cut-flower arrangements or bulbs in plain glass vases with moss, sand, or coloured gravel. For a large venue some huge branches of pink cherry blossom in tall vases or a single tall orchid in a clear vase can also work really well.

For a summer wedding you could have gorgeous white hydrangeas (although cut hydrangeas do not travel well, so take that into consideration), peonies and roses, all of which can be bulked out with inexpensive greenery. September brides can do a harvest theme with bright blue cornflowers and lemons or end-of-season lavender plants. And it's easy to do flowers for a winter wedding on a budget using holly, ivy, candles and red berries, or red poinsettias in wreaths or pots.

You don't need to buy masses of flowers – a big, tall vase with one or two striking flowers can be simple, yet stunning. Also, it works out much cheaper to buy a larger quantity of one type of flower than to buy smaller numbers of different ones. Flowers like roses or tulips that flop a little can be a good option on a budget as they create an impression of more volume for less.

Buy your flowers a couple of days in advance to allow the buds to open in time, and if they don't, take a tip from the professionals and coax them gently with a hairdryer to make them open.

Look at florists' websites for inspiration, or check out the way they do things in Thailand. They make floating flowers and flower petals into an art form, so you could do some table decorations on the cheap that will be real talking points. Small table arrangements of white and green flowers in glass vases, surrounded by tealights and placed on mirrors can be extremely effective.

If you don't have any luck with the flower markets, try your local garden centre instead. It's amazing how many pots of lavender or hydrangeas you can pick up cheaply, then all you need to do is beg, borrow or hire some containers, or dress up the pots they are in with pretty paper, cloth and ribbon.

For a vintage theme, fill old-fashioned teapots, teacups or bowls with bulbs – hyacinths work well – and then top them with moss for an interesting display. And you can give these away at the end of the evening to friends and family.

## Tables

If you are having a sit-down meal it is worth allocating money to the tables as this is where people spend most of the wedding, sitting, chatting, eating and listening to speeches. You don't need lots of party favours, but comfortable chairs are a good investment, as are pretty flowers and candles (not too high so that people can see each other across the table) and some tasty food.

## Food

Don't waste money here and keep it simple. Inexpensive, traditional foods like sausages and mash, shepherds' pie, and crumble served with champagne is always trendy. Simple, but well executed works much better than flashy and fussy. If you are not having a sit-down do, it's cheaper to do things like canapés. You just need to make sure there are plenty of them, that they are presented in a bold way (served on mirrors is a good trick), and that's it's all dished up by great staff.

You might also want to think about having a wedding brunch or a tea. An afternoon wedding followed by a great tea, champagne, sandwiches, scones and wedding cake, will keep your costs down and allow you to slope off early for a quiet *diner à deux* or to catch an evening flight for your honeymoon.

### Wedding cake

For a traditional cake, get a local cook to make and ice a cake, then spend the rest of your wedding cake budget on fabulous ready-made decorations to put on top of it. Or think about cupcakes, in pretty white cases with white icing and a rose petal or a sprinkle of glitter dust. Piled high, they are a great alternative, and always really popular (plus you can serve them as a pudding and cut down on catering costs).

If a tiered cake will break the budget, another idea is to go for a simple cake for the wedding couple, plus one cake per table, then when the bride and groom cut theirs, so does one person at each table. It's less expensive and it gets everyone involved.

## Music

Save money by not booking a band or a DJ. Just load up an iPod with a whole event's worth of music that you love, that is suitable for all ages and that creates the mood you want. Then, simply plug it in to some speakers and the party is under way.

## Photographs

Put an ad up in a local college that runs photography courses for a talented amateur to take the pictures of your big day. Look at the student's portfolio beforehand to make sure you like their style and go for some wonderful, original shots instead of the more traditional type.

If you are set on having a professional photographer, book them for just half a day to take your formal shots only, and then get your bridesmaids, ushers and family to take plenty of pictures of the reception using colour or black and white disposable cameras provided by you.

Think twice before spending money on having your day filmed. Most people never watch their wedding DVD, and it is a big expense – you are better off putting the money towards something essential.

## Honeymoons

When you are booking your honeymoon make sure you check when it's high or low season in your desired location. You might get a better deal with a hotel if you book direct with them, rather than through an agent, and if you go in mid- or low season. Obviously you don't want to book a honeymoon in the Maldives if you can only afford to go when it is raining, but find out exactly what the weather conditions are in your dream location and look at low-season prices there. In many tropical locations the rainy season may just mean a torrential rainstorm for an hour in the afternoon, while the rest of the day is sunny and warm, so it's worth doing thorough research into this. Email the hotel itself and ask someone who is actually there for weather reports, rather than relying on a travel agent at home.

Look at breaking up your journey and flying to places where many different carriers operate; that way you could use a smaller airline for one leg of your journey, benefiting from more competitive prices. You only honeymoon once (hopefully) so get it right, and at the best price.

## Let your friends help out

Get your friends to help out by assigning a job to each of them. One can source cheap drink deals, another can organise getting hold of glassware, while another can hire crockery and cutlery. And you can give a prize to the one who saves you the most money!

# A new baby

Having a new baby is a wonderful time in your life, but it can also be a massive expense, if you are not careful. And if it is your first baby, you may well be confused as to what you do and do not really need.

If friends are throwing a baby shower for you, put together a list of things that you are going to use, and ask the prospective grandparents to club together for more expensive items.

Here is our Spendsmart priority list for buying the new-baby essentials:

## Do spend on:

- a good car seat (or if a friend has one to give you that's fine, but don't buy second-hand in case it has been in an accident)
- plain Babygros – choose plain white cotton ones that can withstand repeated washing; when the baby gets too long for them you can cut the feet off the clothing
- a neutral colour paint for the baby's room, to which you can add and change themed accessories as the baby grows up, rather than spending money on redecorating
- a good cot mattress; second-hand cots are fine, but you will probably want a new mattress

- a sealable bin for dirty nappies
- a first-aid kit, including a thermometer
- a baby monitor
- a good brand of sunscreen
- an electric breast pump – these are the only ones that really work
- a wipeable changing mat.

## Don't spend on:

- an expensive designer buggy
- formula and sterilising units – breastfeeding is free
- jars of baby food – it's so easy (and more nutritious) to make purées yourself and freeze them in ice-cube trays
- designer baby clothes –they last for such a short length of time and are not worth buying
- baby wipes – before these were invented people managed perfectly well with cotton wool and a saucer of warm water
- designer nursery gear – another unnecessary expense with which you will get fed up and the baby will grow out of in no time
- breastfeeding pillows – an ordinary pillow is fine
- expensive chairs for feeding – again, any comfortable chair does the job
- bath and body products for newborns; a little olive oil in the bath is all they really need.

Join up to baby clubs in stores – many of them have giveaways and vouchers for new parents-to-be, so sign up for any freebies that are on offer.

# Buying gifts

When it comes to buying gifts, it's all in the planning and in using your imagination.

## Birthday gifts

You'll find lots of suggestions for what to buy and where in the Spendsmart Directory, whether you are buying for a designer-label addict, an eco-conscious mate or a member of your family. Always remember, though, that the best gifts are those that have been thought about, and it's always wise to buy what a person really loves, rather than what you think they should have or love.

## Wedding gifts

You don't have to buy something expensive from a list, especially as it is not always that exciting buying a toaster or a rubbish bin!

Why not give the wedding couple a surprise on their big day: use a photo editing programme on your computer to print out sepia shots of them, cut out their faces, mix them with little circles of pink (or any colour) tissue paper and put them in bags. Then hand these out to guests to throw as confetti for a wonderful, personal touch.

Or you could volunteer to take some reportage-style black and white shots of the couple's big day and put them in an album, along with messages from friends and family, for when they get back from their honeymoon.

Another lovely idea is a small tree (or pair of trees) to mark the day – a unique, but very reasonable gift. Or you could collect a favourite recipe from each guest at the wedding and get them bound into a personalised book.

Club together with some friends to get some Eastern night lights. Traditionally used in festivals in the Far East, these beautiful lanterns are released into the sky with wishes or greetings written on them, and are a spectacular site to behold.

Luggage tags might not sound like the most thrilling present, but over 250,000 people lose their luggage every month, and that can really spoil things if it happens on a honeymoon.

Lastly, why not buy the couple a beautifully bound volume of love poems to read to each other on honeymoon – a truly romantic gift.

## New baby gifts

For a great baby gift on a budget, try one of these:

- Get the baby's initials embroidered on a plain towel or blanket.
- Buy some of your old favourite children's books at a vintage or car boot sale and tie them up as a set with pale pink or blue ribbon.
- Gift boxes for new mums that can be delivered direct to the hospital or home.

## Christmas gifts

As a general rule, try to buy in unusual stores so people are less likely to know what you have spent. Avoid big stores and find fun things like stockings or reindeer candles in one-off boutiques or travelling Christmas fairs.

Here are a few ideas for unusual and inexpensive presents.

- Buy a box of six ornaments and put some personalised ribbon through each of them (companies that do children's name labels offer this service).
- If you enjoy cooking, make a Christmas cake, pudding or

mince pies and tie them up in white cotton with a single sprig of holly for extra festive chic.

- Buy inexpensive plain glass storage jars and fill them with home-made cookies or Christmas shortbread. Alternatively, fill them with personalised M&M's in festive colours.

- Track down a Christmas market in the nearest city and buy stollen, heart-shaped gingerbreads and other fun, inexpensive goodies there. Plan an outing there with friends and share the petrol costs.

- A great family picture in a simple frame always goes down well with parents. Or burn a CD of carefully chosen Christmas music that you know the person will love. It can be a Christmas carols selection for an auntie, or a Rat Pack retro compilation for your dad.

- Buy a vintage film poster and have it framed – they look great in modern homes.

- Buy a classic Christmas DVD for a friend – it's amazing how many people have never seen *White Christmas* or *It's a Wonderful Life*.

- Looking ahead to the regulation January detox, a clear glass mug filled with flowering jasmine tea buds that open when you pour boiling water on them makes a great present.

- Star- or festively shaped cookie cutters can be bought very cheaply in local kitchenware shops – just tie them up with pretty ribbon and a candy cane and give to someone who loves to bake.

- Plant an amaryllis in a simple pot, with moss on the top for a professional look. Wrap in simple, clear cellophane and tie with raffia or ribbon.

- Make your parents or siblings a yearbook filled with pictures of where you went together, mementos of trips, holidays and birthdays, or whatever you fancy. They will love it.

- Make a voucher for a friend – choose a piece of coloured paper and write on it, 'This voucher entitles you to come shopping with me in the sales where I will spend £X on something you really, *really* want!'
- For children, take a look at the 'used' selection of toys on websites like Amazon. You can buy items that have barely been touched and are still in their original packaging for half the price.
- Think about buying presents for a whole family, rather than individuals. Theme a hamper to their taste, or for the family with a sweet tooth check out online sweet shops and choose a box full of their favourites, retro and new.

# Travel

## Home swapping

Doing a home swap – be it national or international – with another family is an easy way to cut your holiday costs. One of the advantages of having decluttered your home is that you can now take some photographs of it looking great, to show to other prospective home swappers. Do go through a specialist company or website to ensure that you are swapping with people who have been vetted; you may be charged a small introduction fee for this service but it is worth it.

You can swap with couples or families anywhere in the world – the USA, Australia and Canada are particularly well practised at this – and it makes managing your holiday budget so much easier if all you have to pay for are your flights.

## In the UK

Why not look into some of the National Trust properties where you get to spend time in great places and do some work for the Trust. The jobs can vary, as can the accommodation – from lighthouses to basic hostel-type huts – but if you really need a holiday, and can adopt the change-is-as-good-as-a-rest philosophy, this could work well for you. Alternatively, look into booking a holiday on a farm where you can get away and get close to nature at the same time!

### London

If you are thinking of a stay in London, find out about universities that rent out their halls of residence in the holidays (from mid-June to mid-September) at a very reasonable rate. Also, check out deals on tourist attractions before you hit the capital and look out for vouchers for up to 20 per cent off admission prices to some of them.

## Europe and beyond

Don't just accept a quoted price for a holiday or a flight. This is a business involving complicated, multi-layer pricing systems, and it is not uncommon to find that everyone in a given hotel has paid a different rate for the same holiday. So you want to be sure that you've got it for less!

Consider going away for one week, rather than two. This may sound drastic, but paying for a holiday on a budget does involve making choices. Also, think about taking the family away in the May half-term week, rather than in the summer holidays. Many countries have good weather at that time and you will pay much less to travel then. Flying mid-week can also work out significantly cheaper than setting out at the weekend.

If you are dealing with a travel agent, ask them about IT (inclusive tour) deals, in which long-haul flights are sometimes sold with a few nights' accommodation at no extra cost. Also, look into getting cheaper flights by making a stopover somewhere. For example, travelling from London to Los Angeles might work out much more reasonable if you fly via Holland.

When you are looking at flight prices, make sure you factor in the extra charges. You might think that tickets with the bigger airlines and scheduled flights are more expensive, but once you've added charges for check-in, baggage, priority boarding and credit-card booking fees, the 'cheap' flights are not always so cheap!

Some of the no-frills airlines do not provide meals and charge a lot of money for inferior snacks, so it pays to buy something in the departure lounge instead.

It's also important to think about costs once you have reached your destination. Flights to Thailand might be more expensive than those to Italy, but when it comes to spending two weeks there, it is definitely less. Do your research – countries like India, Africa and Vietnam are all really cheap to stay in, so make sure you know the cost of living wherever you are planning to go. In 2008, Bulgaria was the cheapest European country to holiday in, followed by Turkey and Spain, while France, Portugal and Italy were the most expensive. But all of this changes, so keep a close eye on where you can get the most for your money.

A self-catering holiday will always be cheaper than one in a hotel and you can take some of the basics with you (like washing powder, teabags and coffee, all of which can be expensive abroad).

A villa with a pool works out more expensive than one without. Choose one that is really near to the beach instead, so that you can go there for swimming every day. Also, look into going away with friends. This can work well, especially with families whose children are the same ages as yours, and can cut the cost of accommodation, as booking a villa always works out cheaper if there are more of you.

Eat the local food rather than the tourist specials, as this will be the best option price-wise. And ask locals for restaurant recommendations, rather than using a guidebook.

If you decide to stay in a hotel, check out the comparison websites, and always look hotels up on one of the travel review sites so that you know your money will be well spent.

Never use anything from a hotel minibar; buy alcohol in Duty Free and snacks and bottled water from a local shop. And don't pay more for a hotel deal that includes breakfast. Unless you are staying in the middle of nowhere, breakfast at a local café will always be cheaper and probably much nicer than a hotel buffet.

If you hire a car on holiday in Europe, choose one that takes diesel, and fill up at the big supermarket petrol stations, as they are generally cheaper than those on the motorways. On your car-hire agreement, never tick the option for the rental company to refuel the car when you take it back. Make sure you fill it up yourself to avoid paying over the odds.

Lastly, do clock up air miles whenever and wherever you can. These can always be put to good use when it comes to planning next year's holiday!

## Avoid paying bank charges abroad

Be aware of how much it can cost to use your debit and credit cards abroad, and don't get caught out. Credit card fees abroad are higher than debit cards' for cash withdrawals. If you want to avoid fees altogether then look into getting a card that carries no foreign exchange fees or charges on cash advances. Do not change money at airports or ferry terminals, do it before you go.

## Train travel

Trains have become a bit like planes; everyone in your carriage will have paid a different amount for their ticket.

In general it pays to plan ahead with train travel, as the sooner you buy your ticket the cheaper it should be. Don't be afraid to ask at the station or look online to check what the cheapest Apex fare is, and try to get that rate. If your train journey takes you through a mainline station it can sometimes pay to split your journey, so that you buy a single up to that station, and then another ticket from there to your final destination.

Think about going by coach, too. It may take longer, but this is reflected in the price and can be a good option on a budget.

# Christmas

## Planning ahead

If ever there was anything that benefits from planning ahead, it is food shopping for Christmas. It is so easy to go over budget on this, so don't think it is too soon to get the shopping started in October, and pace yourself.

If you are hosting a Christmas do, put a few extra things in your shopping trolley every week. Choose items with a long shelf life – you could buy just one box of shortbread the first week, then a bottle of brandy, and jars of pickle and various trimmings, without going over budget if you start in October.

## Decorations

Raid your garden or local woods for greenery, then pile it up on windowsills or wind it around a circular wire frame to make a wreath with some fairy lights intertwined.

Check out stores for great paper garlands that you can string across the room; there is a great choice these days of snowflakes, doves and hearts. Or get your children involved in preparing decorations – they love to make old-fashioned paper chains and glittery stars, which are cheap, fun and effective ways to make your home look festive.

Most garden centres and shops put their Christmas decorations on sale a week or so before Christmas, so it can be worth waiting until then to buy them. Choose a colour scheme and stick to it – it's more cost-effective to buy big boxes of silver, red or blue baubles than to buy them all individually or in smaller numbers. Look out for large, clear glass baubles and make them special by putting green and silver Christmas trees in each one (from cake decorator suppliers), then tie them to your tree with some red ribbon and add a white luggage label to each, with 'Merry Christmas' written in gold or silver ink.

Simple church candles look fabulous on a mantelpiece with silver baubles. Or you could create snow globes with the children and use them as decorations or to give away as presents. Simply place a small object inside a jam jar (little wooden houses or toy soldiers are ideal), fill with glitter and water and screw the lid on tightly.

Americans thread long lines of popcorn together using a needle and strong cotton to hang as garlands on Christmas trees. Make an afternoon's activity of it by buying some popping corn and doing it with the kids on a cold afternoon. They last for weeks.

Wrap white cotton or muslin around clementines or tennis balls (or anything round that you happen to have in the house), so that they look like little Christmas puddings, which you can then attach to your tree along with some white fairy lights.

Why not try making your own dried citrus slices? Buy a load of oranges and grapefruits from the supermarket and, using a really sharp knife, cut them into thin slices and arrange them on baking sheets. Place them in the oven on its lowest setting and, with the oven door ajar, leave them in for about six hours. (Do not shut the door as the slices will steam and go soggy.) Your house will smell fabulous by the end of the six hours, after which you can take out the slices and leave them somewhere warm for about two days to dry out completely.

## Trees

This is one area where it pays to wait, as the later you leave it to buy your tree, the cheaper it will be. Go with a couple of friends and some cash at closing time, as traders will sometimes take a cash deal for two or three at the end of the day. Also, ask them whether they are selling offcuts – they can be really useful to put on mantelpieces or to make wreaths and you can get a pretty big bundle for next to nothing.

Be aware of what you are paying for when it comes to trees. They are usually priced per foot but also depending on type, so make sure you know one fir from another:

- Nordman fir – the original Christmas tree with non-drop needles.
- Fraser fir – similar to the Nordman, but with more branches and less wide at the bottom, so better if space is limited.

- Douglas fir – light green and a wonderful smell; not available every year.
- Scots pine – a great smell and also good at retaining its needles.
- Blue spruce – silver blue in colour with very bushy, luxurious branches.

Whichever type of tree you go for, make sure you add some warm water and a tablespoon of honey to the pot it stands in – this should help to extend its life and delay needle shedding.

## Food

If you are hosting Christmas, make sure you don't over-cater. Get people to confirm whether or not they are coming before you go shopping for turkeys and other big items. Ask others to contribute, so that one person brings the champagne, another brings the Christmas pudding, you do the main course, and so on.

Presentation is important when it comes to Christmas food. Icing sugar dusted over brownies gives them a festive look, or you can mix it with glitter sugar from cake shops and sprinkle on to plates of bargain truffles or mince pies to make them look a little more glamorous. Buy a few bags of tealights and scatter them in among the food on the dining table – it is cheaper than buying big candles and can look really pretty.

## Drinks

Ask each of your guests to bring a bottle. Also, see pp. 196–7 for advice on party cocktails – especially important at Christmas when people seem to drink double the amount they usually do. Mulled wine is easy; and the cinnamon and orange flavours allow you to choose a cheaper red wine without anyone noticing the difference, add some apple juice to the mix to make it go further. You can also disguise cheaper vodkas with a flavour.

## Gifts

Start well in advance of Christmas by making a list of all the people you need to buy gifts for, with a price by each name of how much you want to spend. As with the Christmas food shopping (see p. 216), try to buy a gift per week from October onwords and put your purchases in a drawer or cupboard. Also, if you see things during the year that would make good Christmas presents, or when you are on holiday, buy them and keep them in your designated cupboard until December.

Don't get in a panic about buying expensive gifts – it is just not worth it. For great ideas for Christmas gifts on a budget, see pp. 210–12.

## Cards

Look out for Christmas cards in the January sales, when you can pick them up really cheaply, then keep them in a drawer until you need them in December. Or, if you want to be creative, buy a pack of plain white cards from any stationery shop and stick just about anything you want onto them – photographs, glitter, felt, holly leaves – to create fun and original cards. Look on the Internet for unusual card ideas.

## Gift wrap

Buy your Christmas gift wrap in bulk and make sure you get good value for money. Rolls work out more economical than sheets, but check labels to see how much paper is on a roll, as lengths can vary. Alternatively, buy plain brown paper and personalise it either by tying dried oranges onto the ribbon, using different coloured raffia from garden centres or florists, or getting your children to decorate it with crayons and glitter.

Don't waste paper trying to wrap really big presents – either get a specially made present sack, or simply tie an enormous bow around the gift. Cut up old cards with pinking shears to create instant gift tags. Or print out smaller ones on your computer: just type in a festive message in different fonts, sizes and colours, copy and paste to fill the page and print out using a colour printer.

## The real spirit of Christmas

If the whole Christmas thing is too much for you, why not tell all your friends and family that you've decided to give it a miss this year, and volunteer your services instead at www.survivingchristmas.co.uk, so that you can help others who are much worse off than yourself.

## Spendsmart summary

### Benjamin and Jay

Throughout the Spendsmart process you have been constantly referred back to getting deeper into your issues in order to get out of debt and/or negative spending habits. If you've done that successfully, you'll be really well set up now for making changes. So well done! It's takes real courage to start looking at the world as being partly a consequence of who you are in it, rather than just what it does to you. It means you are taking responsibility for yourself, which is a key part of personal growth.

As you put your plan into action over the next few weeks and months, you should find that a greater sense of fulfilment begins to emerge for you around money. You may find that your life becomes more grounded and that you start to engage in more meaningful activities, conversations and relationships. These are all now available to you because you are no longer using money as something to hide your deeper self behind.

As you start to change, you will find that things and people around you will change, too. Of course this was not your direct aim in becoming Spendsmart – that would be a doomed strategy – but if you genuinely alter yourself, change around you is inevitable. Some of these other changes might be difficult, sudden or unpleasant for you at first, and you will need to be brave enough to let them take their own course. An internal clearout must, of necessity, involve some external rebalancing and adjusting.

So, as you stand at the threshold of your new Spendsmart life, you are now ready for a new you and a new existence. It might seem a bit daunting at first, but it's going to be a more secure life with a plan and a sense of knowing where you are going, how you are going to get there and why. You have set yourself a challenge, and now you are going to live up to it. You can defeat your anxieties and stare confidently into the future knowing that you have a plan, that you will stick to it and that you can cope with whatever comes up along the way.

You have begun your Spendsmart journey. Enjoy the trip.

# The Spendsmart Directory

## Step one – Spendsmart Reality

### Information on financial products

For all your financial needs check out www.moneysupermarket. com. It compares financial products to show you where to find the best rates for borrowing, the best credit card transfer deals and the lowest APRs around. It can also help you to find the best bank account for your situation. Also, check out www.find.co.uk for more advice and information on bank accounts.

Another great resource for all financial products is www.moneyextra.com, and check out www.about-credit-cards. co.uk for specialist credit card advice. For advice on student loans go to www.direct.gov.uk.

### Information on unauthorised bank charges

If you feel that your bank has charged you unfairly, go to the following sites to find helpful tips, advice and information on fighting back:

www.bankchargeshell.co.uk
www.bankactiongroup.co.uk
www.penaltycharges.co.uk

## Advice on debt

When it comes to seeking help and advice with sorting out your debts the National Debt Helpline and the Consumer Credit Counselling Service are the only people to talk to. They know what they are doing, are approachable and friendly and have your best interests at heart.

The National Debt Helpline 0808 808 4000
Mon–Fri, 9 a.m.–9 p.m., Sat 9.30 a.m.–1 p.m.
www.nationaldebtline.co.uk

The Consumer Credit Counselling Service (CCCS)
0800 138 1111
Mon–Fri 8 a.m.–8 p.m.
www.cccs.co.uk

## Mortgage advice

Go to www.moneynet.co.uk to find the best mortgage rate for you. For mortgage arrears advice, download the FSA advice booklet 'What to do when you can't pay your mortgage' at: www.moneymadeclear.fsa.gov.uk/pdfs/mortgage_can'tpay. pdf. Also check out: www.adviceguide.co.uk and www. payplan.com.

## Independent financial advice

Independent Financial Advisers (IFAs) are regulated by the Financial Services Authority, and are the only type of financial advisers who can give you unbiased advice about all the products available in the marketplace to make sure you get the right product for your specific needs. Find one at www.unbiased. co.uk or www.sesame.co.uk.

## Main UK credit reference agencies

These are the main UK credit reference agencies and for a nominal fee you are entitled to see what they have listed about you and your credit rating:
www.equifax.co.uk
www.callcredit.co.uk
www.experian.co.uk

# Step two – Spendsmart Preparation

## Selling and swapping

For general information on swapping check out
www.freecycle.org
www.swapitshop.com
www.swapxchange.com and www.whatsmineisyours.com

If you think you might want to become a car booter, check out local sales on www.carbootcalendar.com or
www.carbootjunction.com – and be prepared to get up early! To check out renting something you might need rather than buying it, go to www.zilok.co.uk.

Books and DVDs sell well second-hand on
www.amazon.co.uk and www.ebay.co.uk. Or, if you have loads of books to get rid of, try www.greenmetropolis.com. If you want to swap or sell clothes, try www.bigwardrobe.com. For all other items and furniture check out the following:

www.musicmagpie.com
www.ebay.co.uk
www.cqout.com
www.ebid.net
www.qxi.co.uk
www.flogitall.com
www.easy2sell.biz
www.trading4u.com
www.gumtree.com
www.preloved.co.uk
www.flogit4u.com

# Landline, TV and mobile resources

The best comparison websites for checking out landline and broadband deals are www.uswitch.com and www.firsthelpline. com. For more specific information on phone and TV deals, check out the websites below.

## National call override providers

www.saynotoo870.com – provides alternative numbers for many major companies
www.callchecker.com – checks out the best deal for whoever you are calling and from any phone.

## International call override providers

For international calls at cheap rates check out:
www.Vyke.com
www.jajah.com
www.globedialler.com
www.speaktotheworld.co.uk

## Cheap calls

www.skype.com

## Digital TV comparison sites

www.uswitch.com

www.digital-tv.co.uk

www.digitalchoices.co.uk

## Mobile phone tariffs comparison sites

www.onecompare.com

www.mobilephonechecker.co.uk

www.moneysupermarket.com

## Selling your old mobile

www.envirofone.com

www.onecompare.com

www.mobilephonechecker.co.uk

www.fonebank.com

www.mazumamobile.com

www.findyourgooseberry.com

## International phone cards

www.planetphonecards.com

www.thephonecardsite.com

## Stand-alone SIM cards

www.oneroam.co.uk

www.GoSim.com

www.Sim4travel.com

www.noodle.co.uk

www.storytelecom.com

www.letsroam.com

www.simply-fone.com

## Unlocking your mobile phone

www.unlockNokiafree.com

www.Unlockitfree.com

www.mobilefreedom.co.uk

www.unlockme.co.uk

# Utilities

## Price comparison websites for utilities

www.energyhelpline.com

www.energylinx.com

www.moneysupermarket.com

www.simplyswitch.com

www.uswitch.com

www.ukpower.com

www.energywatch.org.uk

www.switchwithwhich.co.uk

## Energy-saving devices

For websites that sell Wattson devices (which are the devices that connect to your fuse box and display your energy usage) check out www.diykyoto.com, www.electricity-monitor.com and www.properprice.co.uk. For lots of energy saving products and services visit www.britisheco.com.

## Car costs

### Car insurance price comparison websites

www.comparethemarket.com

www.confused.com

www.gocompare.com

www.moneysupermarket.com

www.tescocompare.com

www.uswitch.com

www.insuresupermarket.com

## Home insurance

### Home insurance price comparison websites

www.insuresupermarket.com

www.gocompare.com

www.comparethemarket.com

www.confused.com

www.moneysupermarket.com

# Step three – Spendsmart Detox

## Substitutes for shopping

For ideas of charities to get involved with which might pair your interests up with what's needed out there, check out www.timebank.org.uk.

## Price comparison websites

www.shopzilla.com
www.pricegrabber.com
www.become.com
www.kelkoo.co.uk
www.ciao.co.uk
www.moneysupermarket.com
www.pricerunner.co.uk
www.uk.shopping.com
www.nextag.co.uk

# Step four – Spendsmart Budget

## Help with preparing your budget

### Letter templates

www.nationaldebtline.co.uk
www.cccs.co.uk

### Impartial consumer advice

www.which.co.uk

## Making extra money

### Extras

www.Nasaa.org.uk
www.thecastingsuite.co.uk
www.2020casting.com
www.extras.co.uk

## Skills

www.peopleperhour.com
www.setyourrate.com
www.peopleperhour.com

## Mystery shopping

www.retaileyes.co.uk
www.cyber-shop.gfk.com
www.storecheckers.co.uk
www.mysteryshop.org

# Children on a budget

Are your kids are bored with their games? Instead of buying them a new one, why not try the following game-swapping site: www.cubebeater.com. For lots of ideas on free stuff to amuse and entertain, try out www.dofreestuff.com. For second-hand children's shopping look at www.loopkids.co.uk. For a fun day out try your hand at fruit picking: www.pickyourown.org.uk.

# Store points

Here are the main reward schemes and the best ways to use them:

www.tesco.com/clubcard. Rather than redeem the vouchers that you get in store, use them on deals listed in the store's brochure. Magazine subscriptions and admission to family attractions like Alton Towers are regularly featured.

www.nectar.com – this card awards points for shopping in Sainsbury's, Debenhams, BP and TalkTalk, among others. Claim your points and use for DVD rental vouchers, restaurants, Eurostar and theme parks.

www.boots.com – points can be redeemed on most things in the store. Watch out for in-store and online double- or treble-your-points offers.

## Cashback Sites

www.froggybank.co.uk
www.topcashback.co.uk
www.Quidco.co.uk
www.Greasypalm.com

# Car costs

## Lowest price local petrol

www.petrolprices.com – find the lowest petrol price in your area.

## Car ad companies

To make money while you're sitting in traffic check out: www.ad-wraps.co.uk and www.comm-motion.co.uk.

## Car clubs

If you occasionally need to use a car, but don't want the expense involved with running your own, why not check out the car clubs, at www.streetcar.co.uk, www.citycarclub.co.uk and www.carclubs.org.uk.

Also, take a look at www.liftshare.org. This is an online national network of car sharing, aimed at making more efficient use of millions of empty car seats; just log in your journey and the site links you up with others who are taking the same route and with whom you can get a lift.

# Food – shopping, cooking, eating out and drinking on a budget

## Supermarkets online

www.fixtureferrets.co.uk

www.mysupermarket.co.uk

## Farmers' markets nationwide

www.farmersmarkets.net

## Organic delivery companies

www.abel-cole.co.uk

www.caleyco.com

www.freshfood.co.uk

www.organics-4u.co.uk

## Recipe websites

www.jamieoliver.com

www.deliaonline.com/recipies

www.nigella.com

www.bbc.co.uk

www.eattheseasons.co.uk

www.freerecipes.com

www.lovefoodhatewaste.com

## Eating out

www.grabameal.co.uk

www.toptable.co.uk

www.tastelondon.co.uk

www.tasteuk.co.uk

www.5pm.co.uk

www.lastminute.com

## Cheap wine

Majestic Wines and Oddbins have branches nationwide and consistently offer great deals. With Majestic you have to buy a case (twelve bottles) but you can fill it with twelve different bottles, which is really helpful for budgeting. Oddbins have no minimum buy.

Jane MacQuitty consistently suggests good value cheap drinkable wines in her Saturday column in *The Times* magazine (read it online for free). Also, look at:

www.lovethatwine.co.uk
www.pricerunner.com
www.majestic.co.uk
www.oddbins.co.uk.

## DIY and other guides

www.ehow.com
www.ultimatehandyman.co.uk
www.videojug.com
www.howtomendit.com

### Sewing repairs

Superdrug do a cute little sewing machine for £7.99. It's good enough to run up a hem and cope with basic repairs.

## Beauty

Take a look at www.consumerresearchonline.co.uk, where you can sign up to try out new beauty products for free. Also, check out:

www.fragrancescompared.co.uk

www.beautybynadine.com
www.instyle.com
www.cult.beauty.blogspot.com
www.thebudgetfashionista.com.

## Vouchers

www.financedaily.co.uk
www.myvouchercodes.co.uk
www.vouchercodes.com
www.voucherheaven.com
www.latestdiscountvouchers.co.uk
www.madaboutbargains.co.uk

## Clothing – swishing and swapping

www.swishing.org
www.stylewillsaveus.com
www.whatsmineisyours.com
www.hybird.co.uk
www.visaswap.com

## Handbag rentals

www.fashionhire.co.uk
www.handbaghirehq.co.uk
www.bagborroworsteal.com
www.handbagsfromheaven.com
www.erento.co.uk

# Competition websites

www.prizefinder.com

# Keeping fit

www.virtualgym.tv
www.optimallifefitness.com
www.britmilfit.com
www.2.btcv.org.uk
www.localsportsclubs.co.uk
www.afaabd.com

# Cheap entertainment

www.free-dvd-club.com – gets you started with fifty free films
to choose from.
www.bbc.co.uk/whatson/tickets
www.powerhousetv.co.uk
www.blockbuster.co.uk
www.lovefilm.com

## Unlocking DVDs

www.multi-region.co.uk
www.DVD.Unlocking.org.uk
www.dvdexplorer.com
www.dvd-codes.co.uk
www.dvdunlocked.com

## Freebies

In addition to all of the above, take a look at www.gumtree. com and www.craiglist.org – they have advertisements from trainees offering free haircuts, massages, etc. Also, www.freecycle.com introduces you to others who will swap things, www.bigwardrobe.com swaps clothes and www. free-samples.co.uk gives out free toiletries and cosmetics. To download free computer games check out www.freeloader.com, as well as www.last.fm/ for great free music downloads.

Do join up to www.hospitalityclub.com, a worldwide club of people who swap homes, get free holidays and help each other out to save money, and look at www.freebielist.com.

# Step five – Spendsmart Life

## Sales

Most of the big sample sales happen in London, so if you fancy getting in the know, check these sites out:
www.samplesaleslondon.com
www.dailycandy.com
www.fashionconfidential.co.uk
www.billiondollarbabes.com
www.londonfashionweekend.co.uk
www.brandalley.co.uk
www.cocosa.com
www.vente-privee.com
www.secretsales.com
www.LynkU.com

# Your home

## Home inspiration for free

www.elledecor.com
www.livingetc.co.uk
www.homesandbargains.co.uk
www.mydeco.com

## Finding local tradesmen and building materials

www.homepro.co.uk
www.screwfix.com/tradecounters
www.transitiontowns.org

## Designer diffusion home ranges

Look out for designer diffusion ranges. Kelly Hoppen does some great stuff for BHS and John Rocha, Betty Jackson, Jane Packer and Jasper Conran all have fabulous diffusion home ranges at Debenhams.
www.bhs.co.uk
www.debenhams.com
www.homebase.co.uk
www.diy.com

## Shelving

www.ikea.com
www.johnlewis.com
www.next.co.uk

## Walls

www.atlantisart.co.uk
www.osborneandlittle.com

www.designersguild.com
www.cathkidston.co.uk
www.fourblankwalls.co.uk
www.55max.com
www.degreeshow.com
www.wills-art.com
www.inspiredartfair.com
www.free-range.org.uk
www.lupegallery.com
www.thephotographersgallery.com
www.photonet.org.uk
www.snapgalleries
www.proud.co.uk
www.minigallery.co.uk
www.britart.com
www.easyart.co.uk
www.thinkpictures.co.uk
www.wonderfulgraffiti.com
www.whatisblik.com
www.marmarco.com
www.nouvellesimages.com
www.acte-deco.fr

## Good designer sale bargains on wallpaper can be found at:
www.janechurchill.com
www.colefax.com
www.designersguild.com
www.osborneandlittle.co.uk
www.cathkidston.co.uk
www.designersguild.com.

## Flooring

www.wickes.co.uk
www.diy.com
www.carpet-express.co.uk
www.homebase.co.uk

## Bedrooms

www.thewhitecompany.com
www.johnlewis.com
www.volgalinen.co.uk

### Under-bed storage

www.ikea.com
www.theholdingcompany.co.uk
www.bagnboxman.co.uk

### Mirrors

www.lauraashley.com
www.ikea.com
www.ilva.com
www.next.co.uk

## Living and dining rooms

### Blinds

www.johnlewis.com
www.ikea.com

### Sofas

www.dwell.co.uk
www.trade-secret.co.uk
www.ikea.com

www.ilva.com

www.bemz.com

### Feature lighting

www.habitat.net

www.dwell.co.uk

www.ikea.com

### Tableware

www.ikea.com

www.habitat.net

www.heals.co.uk

## Kitchens

www.beko.co.uk

www.ikea.com

www.magnet.com

www.discountkitchenfactory.co.uk

www.kitchen-restoration.com

www.diy-kitchens.com

www.yell.com

### For replacement kitchen doors try:

www.kitchenrefurbs.co.uk

www.discountkitchenfactory.co.uk

www.replacementkitchendoors.uk.com

www.mir.excalibur-kitchens.co.uk

## Bathrooms

www.bathstore.com

www.surfacematerialdesign.co.uk

www.brume.co.uk

www.victoriaplumb.com

www.diy.com

## Home office supplies

www.viking-direct.co.uk
www.inkfactory.com
www.cartridgeworld.org
www.cartridgesave.co.uk
www.green-works.co.uk

## Auction houses

www.auctionhammer.co.uk

## Bargains for the home

You're Furnished: 01279 815028
Dunelm Mill: 08451 656565 (www.dunelm-mill.co.uk)
www.trade-secret-club.co.uk
www.homesandbargains.co.uk
www.myhomesense.com
www.matalan.co.uk
www.argos.co.uk
www.kingofcotton.co.uk
www.gumtree.co.uk
www.ebay.co.uk
www.sainsburys.co.uk
www.tesco.com
www.scp.co.uk
www.tkmaxx.com
www.homesense.com
www.national-brands.co.uk
www.dwell.co.uk
www.cli.co.uk

# Your wardrobe

## The best fashion outlet bargains in . . .

### . . . the UK

Bicester Village has labels like Ralph Lauren, Anya Hindmarch, Max Mara, Pringle, Mulberry, Jimmy Choo, Agent Provocateur, to name but a few, and you can join their VIP club online to qualify for further discounts. Bicester really does lead the field but more and more outlets are springing up all over the UK.

### . . . Italy

The legendary Italian discount stores are hard to find but definitely worth the search. In between Florence and Pisa are a host of designer delights. Fendi, Prada, Dolce and Gabbana are all there, plus The Mall which houses Armani, Gucci, Bottega Veneta and Yves Saint Laurent. Expect to get at least 50 per cent off prices of the previous season's collections. Most hotels are used to visitors wanting to explore this increasingly popular shopping route, and should be able to help you with directions.

### . . . the USA

Forget 5th Avenue – if you are in New York get a bus and a coupon book and head out to Woodbury Common. Home to the discount warehouses of Burberry, Chanel, Diana Von Furstenberg, Juicy Couture, Saks, Barneys, True Religion Jeans, Ralph Lauren and Zales diamonds, this is a bargain hunter's dream. It's owned by Premium Outlets who have great outlet centres all over the USA. The other place to note is New England where there is a huge selection of outlet shopping centres including Ralph Lauren and Abercrombie and Fitch.
www.bicestervillage.com
www.mcarthurglen.com

www.gunwharf-quays.com
www.shoppingvillages.com
www.outlet-firenze.com
www.italylimo.com
www.premiumoutlets.com
www.boston.com/travel/exploreene/specials/shopping

## Vintage

www.pa-antiques.co.uk
www.vintagefashionfairs.com
www.carbootcalendar.com
www.retrotogo.com
www.frockmevintagefashion.com
www.rgcshows.com
www.charityshops.org.uk
www.invaluable.com
www.antiques-directory.co.uk
www.antiquesatlas.com
www.alfiesantiques.com
www.visitsouthwark.com/Bermondsey-antiques-market
www.kemptonantiques.com

Oxfam are opening chains of boutiques selling some of their best-quality donations, along with Fairtrade jewellery and unique items that have been customised. They also run mobile shops to tour festivals such as Glastonbury, T in the Park, Woman, and V.

Cancer Research are teaming up with the eco-fashion collective Revamp, and Traid has a new in-house label – Traidremade – so there is a lot going on in the charity world which can only benefit the customer.

# Weddings

Take a look at www.ethicalweddings.com. It was set up by Katie Fewings, a bride who needed to keep costs down, wanted to support local suppliers and, as she puts it, 'give everyone something to celebrate'.

Also worthy of note is www.cheap-wedding-success.co.uk, a website set up by Nicola Ray who says it's easy for modern brides to have a dream day without sacrificing their lifelong dreams to pay for it!

And for inspiration check out:
www.bridesmagazine.co.uk
www.youandyourwedding.co.uk
www.marthastewart.com
www.cheap-wedding-success.co.uk

## Rings

www.cooldiamonds.com
www.ross-simons.com
www.diamonds-usa.com
www.amazon.com
www.abazias.com

## Venues

The American website www.wonderfulgraffit.com will inspire you with all sorts of ideas for your big day. Also, check out www.beautifulworldtents.co.uk for some non-traditional ideas.

## Invitations

www.livingvictorian.com (embosser)
www.threedesigningwomen.com (stamping)
www.paper-source.com
www.deardahlia.com
www.sarahdrakedesign.com
www.paperbuzz.com
www.weddingpaperdivas.com
www.sugarpaper.com

## Dresses and suits

www.thevintageweddingdresscompany.com
www.clothhouse.com

## Flowers

Take a look at www.scentednarcissi.co.uk, who supply narcissi from the Scilly Isles in a range of shades. Or try the Organic Flower Company www.tofc.co.uk, who have been voted the UK's most ethical flower company, bringing in blooms by land and sea, and www.fairtrade.org.uk who source flowers from farms in Kenya, Sri Lanka, Ecuador and Colombia.

Also check out the following top florists for some free inspiration:

www.robbiehoney.com
www.jane-packer.co.uk
www.mcqueens.co.uk
www.paula-pryke-flowers.com.

## Tables

If you're going to do 'favours', check out www.retrosweets.co.uk for old-fashioned favourites that everyone loves, or give little packets of tree or flower seeds from www.wildflower-favours. com. Check out www.weddingfortunecookies.co.uk for personalised treats.

## Food

www.lovefoodhatewaste.com

## Photographs

www.hotcourses.com

## Honeymoons

www.weather.com

# Buying gifts

## Birthday gifts

www.royalmail.com/smilers does a great service whereby you choose the stamp background then upload a photo onto the site and they send you a sheet of personalised stamps. You can put anything from wedding photographs to friends' dogs on them and they are always a huge hit.

Buy an inexpensive simple, chunky glass frame at Muji, Habitat, Ikea or Heals, then put a photograph in it to make a great gift. Or buy a stylish friend their initial in gold or silver from www.poshgraffiti.com or go to www.re-foundobjects.com for large cardboard ones.

For cool kids buy a great retro lunch box by Emma Bridgewater (www.emmabridgewater.co.uk), look at the fabulous recycled cardboard playhouse which you can help decorate from www.ecotopia.co.uk or the rocket playhouse at www.gosseypium.co.uk. Get your child featured in their own story. Go to www.letterbox.co.uk and have a personalised adventure book made for them, which will have their name featured in it, as well as the names of their friends and family, and the name of your town.

Upload photographs and copy and design your own calendar or photo book at www.bobbooks.co.uk – these are a great idea for parents' birthdays or wedding anniversaries.

For chocoholic friends, order the big slabs of chocolate wrapped in bright paper or the half-kilo slabs from www. chococo.co.uk. Eat Your Words do personalised chocolate bars. Choose from photos, messages or get your children to paint a design: www.eat-your-words.co.uk.

And for domestic goddesses get a fabulously packaged box of organic cookie dough, banana bread or carrot cake from www. winonasorganic.com.

For friends who love their homes, check out www.keepcalm-gallery.com. They have a huge collection of typography prints which are modern, cool and very reasonably priced. Why not buy a tree for your green friends at www.treesdirect.co.uk or go to www.carry-a-bag.com for great bags to use instead of plastic ones. Cooks will love the personalised bread rolls that smart French bakery poliane do: www.poilane.fr, or get a personalised jelly mould which gets big votes at children's parties.

Home lovers can send artist David Naylor a picture of their house and he will then paint a watercolour which can be printed onto postcards: www.thepresentfinder.co.uk. Or get them a personalised doormat which can say whatever you want as welcome: www.cotswoldco.com.

Also check out www.firebox.com for your gadget-obsessed friends.

## Wedding gifts

Buy the newlyweds some global luggage tags that can be traced worldwide – visit www.globalbagtag.com. Check out www.wishesinthesky.com for Eastern night lights.

## Baby gifts

Buy a plain towel or blanket and have it embroidered with the baby's initials at www.namesakedesigns.co.uk. Or a lovely, soft stuffed toy or satin-edged pram blanket from www.thewhitecompany.com.

Lullaby Lavender is a great range of all natural baby skincare products which includes the popular bottom balm. They have great packaging and prices are very reasonable. Look for it on www.mintyhen.co.uk.

Great gift boxes for new mums can be delivered direct to the hospital or home from www.babeswithbabies.com.

## Christmas gifts

Never underestimate how kids love their names on things – you can get personalised pencils and pens at www.thepresentfinder.co.uk. For great stockings visit www.qsgroup.co.uk or www.sparrowkids.co.uk who do a stocking kit so you can make your own. You can get reindeer candles at www.notonthehighstreet.com. Also look at www.daylesfordsorganic.com for hampers for the whole family.

www.aquarterof.co.uk for great sweets for the whole family
www.m-ms.com (personalised M&Ms)
www.christmasmarkets.com
www.vintageposter.com
www.allposters.co.uk
www.choitime.com.

# Travel

www.traintravel.com
www.nationalexpress.com
www.megabus.com

## In the UK

www.nationaltrust.org.uk
www.featherdown.co.uk

### London
The London School of Economics have a good choice of budget
accommodation at www.lse-ac.uk.
Also check out:
www.hotels-london.co.uk
www.britainexpress.com
www.discountbritain.net.

## Home swapping

www.homebase-holidays.com
www.homelink.org.uk
www.intervac.co.uk
www.guardianhomeexchange.co.uk

## Travel comparison sites

If you are heading for a city, www.citadines.com and www.interhome.co.uk are good sites for self-catering.

Look at www.couchsurfing.com which will put you in touch with people you can stay with all over the world; and you can also register for people to come and stay at your place.

Good sites for travel bargains:

www.lowcostbeds.com – covers Europe and has now started doing great package deals as well.

www.roomauction.com – covers hotels in the UK and allows you to make an offer on a room.

www.laterooms.com – last-minute deals and hotels at up to 70 per cent off.

Always check with www.tripadvisor.com if you're going to a hotel as it gives you honest reviews by fellow travellers – and no one knows a place better than someone who has just stayed there.

Also look at:

www.expedia.co.uk
www.travelsupermarket.com
www.tvjungle.co.uk
www.tvzoo.co.uk.

## Bank charges abroad

www.payzonemoney.com
www.travelex.co.uk
www.postoffice.co.uk

Find out more about pre-paid cards at www.payzonemoney.com, and for exchanging money use www.travelex.co.uk or www.postoffice.co.uk.

## Contact lenses and glasses

www.contactlenses.co.uk
www.glassesdirect.co.uk
www.lowcostspex.co.uk
www.glassesuk.com

## Christmas

www.janeasher.com
www.re-foundobjects.com
www.prices-candles.co.uk  (seconds store)

### Cards

Visit www.lakeland.com or www.hobbycraft.com for fun slogans or a message of your choice, or check out American sites www.threedesigningwomen.com and www.paper-source.com, www.snowandgraham.com and www.carrotandstickpress.com for more choices than you would ever have believed possible.

### Gift wrap

www.naturalcollection.com
www.christmastimeuk.com
www.viking-direct.co.uk (brown paper)
www.lakeland.co.uk (present sacks)
www.survivingchristmas.co.uk
www.giftclearance.co.uk

# Index